AF386055

Jorge Sá is a senior research fellow at Drucker University (Peter F. Drucker and Masatoshi-Ito Graduate School of Management) in Los Angeles, and a Professor at ISG Business School.

He is an expert on Peter Drucker and Philip Kotler, founders of modern management and modern marketing, respectively, with whom he studied and who have offered letters of recommendation for his books and endorsements for his work.

Has a doctorate (PhD) in Business Administration, from Columbia University and was awarded the Jean Monnet Chair by the Jean Monnet Foundation in Brussels.

His books have been translated into twelve languages and has worked as private consultant, non-executive director or taught in the executive programs of multinational companies, among others, of: Coca-Cola, IBM, Johnson & Johnson, Pfizer, Henkel, McDonald's, UnitedHealth group, Merck, Volkswagen Group and Microsoft.

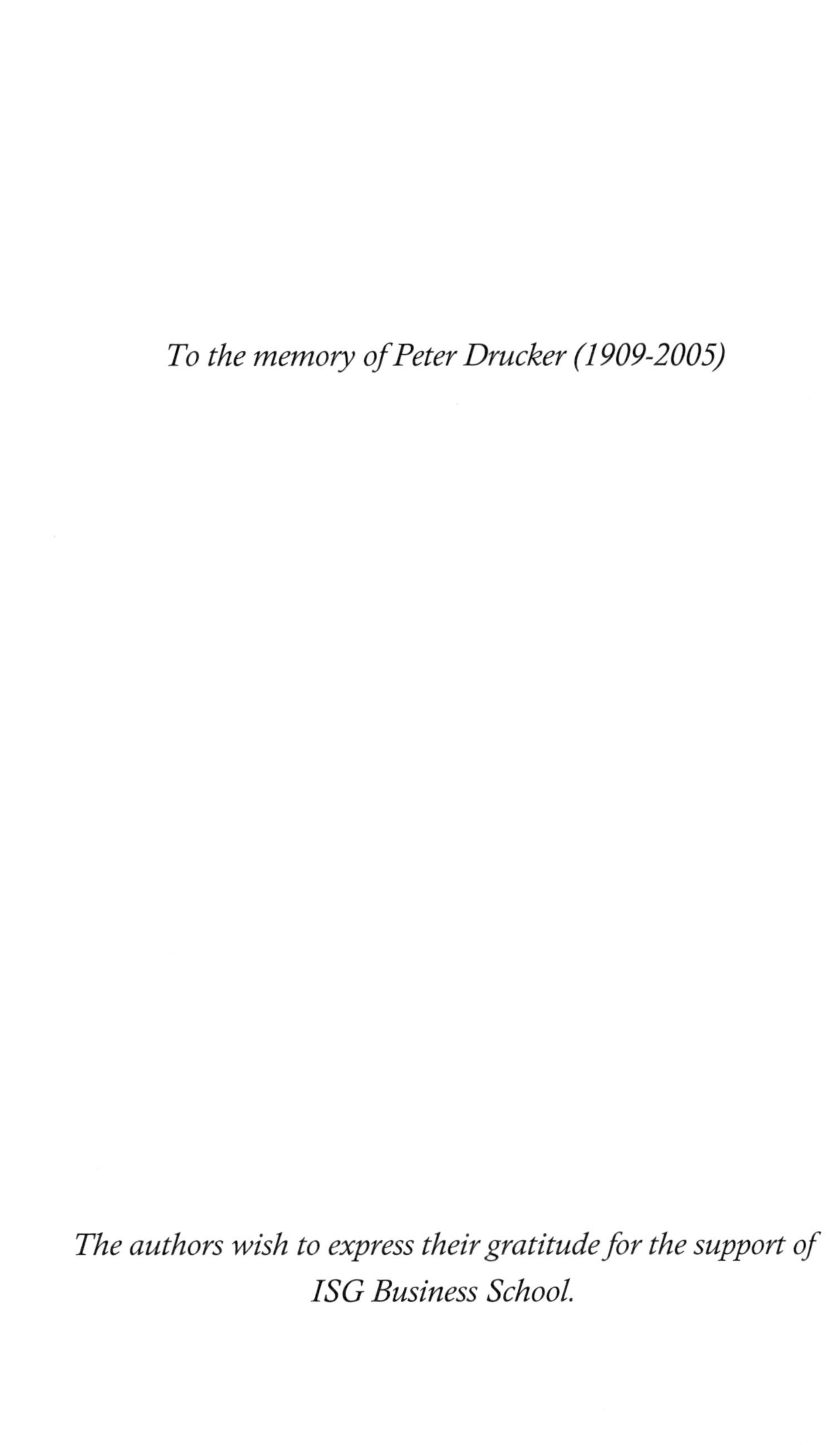

To the memory of Peter Drucker (1909-2005)

The authors wish to express their gratitude for the support of ISG Business School.

Jorge Sá and Paulo Rodrigues and Magda Pereira

ECONOMIC MYTHS AND ECONOMIC REALITIES

Five **mistakes** we are told every single day and the **real sources** of economic growth

AUSTIN MACAULEY PUBLISHERS™

LONDON • CAMBRIDGE • NEW YORK • SHARJAH

Copyright © Jorge Sá and Paulo Rodrigues and Magda Pereira 2024

All rights reserved. No part of this publication may be reproduced, distributed, or transmitted in any form or by any means, including photocopying, recording, or other electronic or mechanical methods, without the prior written permission of the publisher, except in the case of brief quotations embodied in critical reviews and certain other non-commercial uses permitted by copyright law. For permission requests, write to the publisher.

Any person who commits any unauthorized act in relation to this publication may be liable to criminal prosecution and civil claims for damages.

The story, experiences, and words are the author's alone.

Ordering Information
Quantity sales: Special discounts are available on quantity purchases by corporations, associations, and others. For details, contact the publisher at the address below.

Publisher's Cataloging-in-Publication data
Sá, Jorge; Rodrigues, Paulo and Pereira, Magda
Economic Myths and Economic Realities

ISBN 9798889105602 (Paperback)
ISBN 9798889105619 (Hardback)
ISBN 9798889105626 (ePub e-book)

Library of Congress Control Number: 2023921825

www.austinmacauley.com/us

First Published 2024
Austin Macauley Publishers LLC
40 Wall Street, 33rd Floor, Suite 3302
New York, NY 10005
USA

mail-usa@austinmacauley.com
+1 (646) 5125767

Table of Contents

Synopsis of the Book

Economic Myths and Economic Realities: **five** mistakes we are told every single day; and the **real** sources of economic growth.

The book is divided in **two** parts: economic **myths** and economic **realities**.

1. Economic Myths

The **first part** of the book (**economic myths**) presents a few diagrams (from official statistical sources such as EU, IMF, etc.) on **five ideas** that are conveyed daily and are plainly wrong (in some cases), or there is no data, no empirical support for them (in other cases). And thus remain dubious, at best.

Idea	Myth	Reality
First	Large **funding** from the richer to the poorer countries (e.g. within the European Union) promotes competitiveness	In the last quarter of century central funding not only has not avoided, as may have **fostered** corruption and **hampered** economic competitiveness, economic freedom and growth.
Second	Keynesian public **programs** promote growth	The impact of public investment programs is **irrelevant** in a country's short term growth.

Idea	Myth	Reality
Third	Within economic blocks (European Union, USA, etc.) there is a trend towards the **convergence** of countries/federal states	It is the opposite that happens. Countries belonging to **economic unions** tend to **diverge**: their standard of living becomes more different. The wealthier countries become wealthier. Poorer ones, become (relatively) poorer. The same applies to the federal states within the USA.
Fourth	**Gross domestic product** is a good measure of a country's wealth	GDP is an *obsolete concept*. **National income should be used** instead. However, most economists and institutions do not. The World Bank is an exception. Examples from Luxembourg, Ireland, Portugal, etc. explain why.
Fifth	**Industrialization**, that is to increase the manufacturing sector, is the source to create wealth	Aside exceptional cases, there is **no (mathematical) relation** whatsoever, between a country's wealth and the importance of the industry in its economy.

2. Economic realities

The **second part** (on **economic realities**) indicates empirically, using very simple but clear statistics, what the **real sources of economic growth** are. Why the world ten richest countries have **fifty-nine** times the income per capita of the bottom ten. That is, it focuses on the causes of prosperity, which—according to the Nobel Prize winner R. Lucas—are as important as elusive.

To demonstrate the sources of economic progress, the book assumes that the whole of countries (and not only the private sector, but also the public and social sectors) are companies. After all there are many multinationals which are far larger than countries: Walmart, State Grid, Amazon, UnitedHealth, Toyota, to name only a few.

And under that assumption, one is able to explain **90%** of economic growth, that is of variance among countries' wealth.

To demonstrate that, the book uses a sample of 33 countries (both developed and developing), during the five-year period in-between the (end of the) subprime crisis and (the beginning of) the Covid recession and then evaluates the quality of those countries during that period in nine **business administration areas**: 1) strategy, 2) marketing, 3) finance/accounting, 4) human resources, 5) information systems, 6) operations/production, 7) R&D, 8) administrative area (security, hygiene, energy) and 9) general management (objectives, organization, control, coordination).

It is worthwhile to note that the book does not argue that the richest countries have the best firms.

It demonstrates (empirically) that the wealthiest countries **<u>are</u>** the best companies. The whole of the countries—not only the private sector but also the public and social ones—all together outperform the poorer countries in the business functions of human resources management (work ethics, personal ethics, instruction), marketing knowledge, strategy, and so forth.

I Introduction

What most people generally believe
is frequently wrong.

Peter Drucker (founder of modern management)

This book is divided in **two** parts: *myths* and *realities.*

The **first part** of the book presents a few diagrams (from official sources such as EU, IMF, etc.) on **five ideas** that we are daily told and are just plainly wrong (in some cases), or there is no data support for them (in other cases). So, they remain dubious, at best.

And the **second part** indicates empirically what the **real sources of economic growth** are. Why the world ten richest countries have fifty-nine times (!) the income per capita of the bottom ten[1]. That is, it focuses on the causes of prosperity, which—according to the Nobel Prize winner R. Lucas[2]—are as important as elusive.

1.1 The myths

We are daily conveyed **five ideas** which remain at best unproven. They are:

---

[1] Excluding those whose main export is oil, the top ten countries in GDP per capita are: Macao SAR, Singapore, Norway, Switzerland, Hong Kong SAR, Luxembourg, USA, San Marino, Netherlands and Iceland. And the world's bottom ten are Madagascar, Sierra Leone, South Sudan, Liberia, Mozambique, Niger, Malawi, Dem. Rep. of the Congo, Burundi and Central African Republic. The source is the IMF, 2019.
[2] Robert E. Lucas Jr., "On the Mechanics of Economic Development", *Journal of Monetary Economics* 22, no. I (1988): pp. 3-42

First: gross domestic product is a good measure of a country's wealth.

Indeed nowadays[1] GDP is a *misleading concept.* What should be used instead is **national income.** Who uses it? Most economists and institutions do not. The World Bank is an exception.

Second: within economic blocks (European Union, Mercosur, etc.) there is a trend toward the **convergence** of countries, that is for them to become more similar in terms of income. Right?

Wrong: it is the opposite which happens. Countries belonging to **economic unions** tend to **diverge.** Their standard of living becomes more different. The wealthier countries become wealthier. Poorer ones, become (relatively) poorer.

Third: strong **funding** from the richest to the poorest countries can prevent that trend, **correct?**

Wrong again. Funding not only does not avoid that, as may very well **increase** the differences among countries in terms of wealth.

Fourth: what about public **investment,** the so-called Keynesian effect?

Most frequently the impact of public investment programs is **irrelevant** in a country's short term growth.

Fifth: (and finally), some economists argue that the solution is thus the **(re)industrialization,** to increase the manufacturing sector.

---

[1] And even more so into the future.

That is wrong, again. Aside exceptional cases, there is no (mathematical) relation whatsoever, between a country's wealth and the importance of the industry in its economy.

In sum, the **five above statements** are either plainly wrong, or remain at best dubious as no empirical evidence is found to support them.

However, the above is defended by well-known economists, including Nobel laureates, who fall under the so-called *Paul Samuelson* trap, who in several editions of his famous textbook Economic Principles continuously predicted that the Soviet Union GNP would overtake that of the USA, in the next few decades.

Why? The prediction was based on a model called the **production possibility frontier**, which stated that with full employment (the case of the Soviet Union) a country was <u>on</u> and not below (inside the curve) and therefore would be more productive. The pitfall is that the model assumes that all economic systems are...**equally...efficient...** Which of course they are not[1]. Other well-known textbooks *(McConnell s Economics)* repeated the same prediction only this time, even more off-course.

---

[1] Indeed Samuelson presented the analysis and prediction again and again, in every edition of his textbook, except that the overtaking time was always pushed further into the future, starting with the 1964 edition which foresaw Soviet GNP overtaking that of the USA by the mid-1980s—see Paul Samuelson, Economics: An Introductory analysis, 6th ed., New York, McGraw-Hill 1964; pp 807.

Also, in the tenth edition of Economics Samuelson wrote that "it is a vulgar mistake to think that most people in Eastern Europe are miserable" and in the 13th edition of Economics, Samuelson offered up the assertion that "the Soviet economy is proof that, contrary to what many skeptics had earlier believed, a socialist command economy can function and thrive." The same year that version of Economics was published, the Berlin Wall fell. Two years later, the Soviet Union itself became defunct.

And there are many **other paradigmatic examples** of how economic theories fail to describe the world in the absence of important institutional details.

In 1979, Harvard Professor *Ezra Vogel* published a book, *Japan As Number One*[1], which forecasted that Japan would soon become the number one economic power, overtaking all other countries, due to better labor relations, lower crime rates, the quality of its universities and an elite bureaucracy.

Indeed, had Japan continued to grow at its average growth rate of the decade 1963-1973, it would have overtaken the United States in terms of GDP per capita by the mid-eighties and in overall GDP by the end of the nineties. But that did not happen, of course. The growth rate crashed in 1980, the year after Vogel's book came out. And it never really recovered.

Another Nobel Prize winner (in 1987) *Robert Solow* wrote a paper[2] suggesting growth would eventually slow down because as GDP per capita goes up, savings increase and therefore there is more money to invest and more capital per worker. That would make machinery less productive since, in factories now with two machines where there was only one before, the same workers will consequently have to operate both at the same time. A single factory can hire more workers, but the whole economy cannot after its reserve of underused workers is exhausted. Thus each new machine would contribute less and less to GDP and growth will consequently slow down.

---

[1] Japan As Number One: Lessons for America by Ezra Vogel, published by Harvard University Press in 1979.

[2] Robert M. Solow, "A Contribution to the Theory of Economic Growth", Quarterly Journal of Economics 70, no. 1 (1956): 65-94, https://doi.org/10.2307/1884513

Solow's prediction fails, of course, to account for **three** factors. First, *population growth.* Second, there are *other resources* for growth besides (manual) labor and machinery. Most important: intellectual capital, the know-how.

Last, Solow failed to take into account *innovation.* Why should the new (second) machine be as productive as the first one? Why not more sophisticated? Or even automated, thus making superfluous the argument of the scarcity of labor (and consequently that of the diminishing returns).

Although there are many other examples, the relevant question is, why do so often economic models **fail** in their predictions? And the answer is for **two** reasons.

Theories are (over) simplifications of reality. What is just fine. And so they must be based in only a few hypothesis. Fine again. But what they also must do is to be extremely careful in selecting their assumptions to avoid neglecting important aspects of reality.

Still, other times, economists believe that assumptions do not have even to be realistic and all that matters is the formality of the mathematical model.

For instance, *Milton Friedman,* another Nobel Prize winner in a famous 1953 article, argued that the realism of model assumptions was immaterial since mathematical formality allowed for predictions accuracy[1].

That has been contradicted nowadays by an increasingly important new field within economics called **behavioral economics,**

---

[1] Milton Friedman, 1953, The methodology of positive economics, in Essays in positive economics, (Ch 1), 3-43, Chicago, University of Chicago Press.

which has so far given two Nobels, one in 2002 to D. Kahneman and another in 2017 to R. Thaler[1].

More recently, the 2018 Nobel Prize attributed to Paul Romer illustrates again the difficulty to explain the difference in income among countries.

According to Paul Romer and his theory of endogenous growth, wealth is a consequence of profit driven R&D and subsequent public policies which then spread the results.

However, that theory is able to explain only 58% of the variance in income per capita among countries[2] with the reasons for the other 42% of the difference remaining unknown.

That is the focus of the second part of this book: **what are the causes of economic growth?**

1.2 The realities

To demonstrate the sources of economic progress, this book assumes that countries are diversified companies. After all there are many multinationals which are far larger than countries: Walmart, State Grid, Amazon, UnitedHealth, Toyota, to name only a few.

And under this assumption one is able to explain **90%** of economic growth, that is of the variance among countries wealth.

---

[1] Two of the most well-known books of these authors are Thinking Fast and Slow (by D. Kahneman), published by Farrar, Straus and Giroux, 2011; and Misbehaving (by R. Thaler) published by W. W. Norton & Co, 2015.
[2] Paul M. Romer, "Human capital and growth: Theory and evidence", *Carnegie-Rochester Conference Series on Public Policy*, Volume 32 (1990): pp. 251-286.

To demonstrate that, the second part of the book works with a sample of 33 countries (both developed and developing), during the five years period in between the (end of the) subprime crisis and (the beginning of) the Covid recession and then evaluate the quality of those countries during that period in nine business administration areas: 1) strategy, 2) marketing, 3) finance/accounting, 4) human resources, 5) information systems, 6) operations/production, 7) R&D, 8) administrative area (security, hygiene, energy) and 9) general management (objectives, organization, control, coordination).

It is worthwhile to note that the book does not argue that the richest countries have the best firms.

It demonstrates (empirically) that the wealthiest countries **are** the best companies. The whole of the countries—not only the private sector but also the public and social ones and (temporary) non active population—all together outperform the poorer countries in the business functions: in human resources management (work ethics, personal ethics, instruction), marketing knowledge, strategy and so forth.

1.3 Summing up

The **two parts** of the book complement each other.

The first stresses what simply *ain t so*.

Something quite important since in life the problem is not what we don't know (our conscient ignorance); it is not even what we don't know that we don't know (our inconscient ignorance). The greatest problem is what we think that it is, and it ain't so. That misleads us. And thus becomes really dangerous. Those are the **economic myths.**

And then the **second part** of the book focus on the reverse: what is it that *really matters* in terms of creating wealth? The **sources of economic growth**?

Let's then turn to the next pages for the empirical evidence for what it is not, and what really is. Always based in numbers and simple diagrams.

II
Economic Myths: Five Mistakes We Are Told Every Single Day

*In order to dream
we can have no illusions.*

Fernando Pessoa

2.1
Leprechaun Economics: Forget Gross Domestic Product (GDP); Use National Income

What cannot be measured, cannot be managed.

Peter Drucker (founder of modern management)

Leprechauns in Irish folklore are little green bearded men wearing a coat and hat, who in solitude spend their time making and mending shoes and with a pot of gold at the end of the rainbow.

In 2016, *Paul Krugman*, a Nobel Prize winner, alerted in a tweet: Leprechaun economics; Ireland just reported a 26% increase in GDP (gross domestic product).

And then added: it makes no sense; **why** is that in GDP?

The answer is because it **must** be. Because of what GDP means.

Although, as we shall see, the reason for the answer is quite straightforward, the important here is the **question**, exemplifying that nowadays there is something very wrong with GDP as a measure of a country's wealth. And increasingly so into the future, due to the integration of world financial and others markets.

As a result, to measure a country's income, **GDP** must be substituted by another statistic: **national income**.

The World Bank uses it primarily and foremost. However many other international (e.g. Eurostat) and national institutions mostly use the GDP. All resulting in **misleading** the public in general and policy makers and governments in particular, as they lack a true indication of how the economy is actually doing. And in more extreme situations there are no warning signals, no "smoking guns" of dangers ahead. How can one manage what is not adequately measured?

Portugal is an example. In the half decade before going into bankruptcy (and prompting an intervention by the IMF and the European Union), Portugal's GDP per capita converged ± 2,1% with the European Union. Thus the economy seemed to be moving pretty well.

However, in terms of the national income per capita that did not happen. In practice, there was no convergence whatsoever[1]. More. While the gross domestic product per capita increased in those five years by 2,4%, national income per capita augmented by only one fifth of that: less than 0,5%. In both instances the difference was explained by the interests paid to foreigners on an ever-increasing debt.

To see how the use of GDP is today (but not so much in the past) a **dangerous statistic**, let's start by looking at what it means and how it is calculated.

The gross domestic product (**GDP**) is the wealth created within a <u>given</u> geographical area (a country, etc.) during one year. And it can be calculated in two ways.

First, by adding up the value added of all firms, that is the *difference* between their sales and what they buy from the outside (raw materials, parts, components, electricity, etc.)

That difference is the *value added* and corresponds to the payment of all factors of production: salaries to workers, interest to bond

---

[1] The convergence rate was 0,02%.

holders and banks, profits to the shareholders. And to add all these remunerations is the **second** (and obviously equivalent) way to evaluate the GDP.

An important aspect to note is that GDP respects a specific **geography**, such as a country, a region or a federal state. And if we wish to compute the value per capita, all we have to do is to divide it by the number of **residents** in that country.

That is what figure 2-1 shows for the fifteen EU-15 countries (at the moment we write negotiations to conclude the Brexit are still going on, and anyway for the purpose of the analysis the inclusion or not of the UK is irrelevant[1]).

Figure 2-1

Source: AMECO database, June 2019, European Commission

---

[1] PPP in the figure 2-1 title means purchasing power parity and implies adapting the GDP to account for the relative difference of the price of goods (bread, meat, etc.) among countries. All figures next are at PPP too.

The numbers for each country in figure 2-1 were *taken directly from AMECO*, the central statistical office of the European Union, and then converted into a percentage of 100 representing the EU-15 average.

So, Greece's GDP per capita is only 62,8% of the EU-15 average making it the poorest among all European countries; next is Portugal (only 71,6% of the EU- 15 average); then Spain (at 85,8%); and so on.

Two things strike us in figure 2-1. First, the **great difference** in GDP per capita (wealth) among all EU-15 countries.

And, second, when we look at the right hand side of the figure we conclude that **Luxembourg's** GDP per capita is 232,6%, that is 132,6% above the EU- 15 average. Followed by Ireland which at 174,2%, is 74,2% above the average. That makes the GDP per capita of each inhabitant of Luxembourg and of Ireland almost four times $(3,7 = \frac{232,6}{62,8})$ and nearly three times $(2,8 = \frac{174,2}{62,8})$ that of the Greeks, respectively.

Again, note that numbers are extracted directly from the EU (Ameco) database and available by simple consultation (Website: https://ec.europa.eu/ economy finance/ameco/user/serie/SelectSerie.cfm).

However these numbers are as easy to obtain as they are **misleading**, since the values of Luxembourg and Ireland are *grossly inflated* and must thus be corrected to produce the **true, real values of figure 2-2 below.**

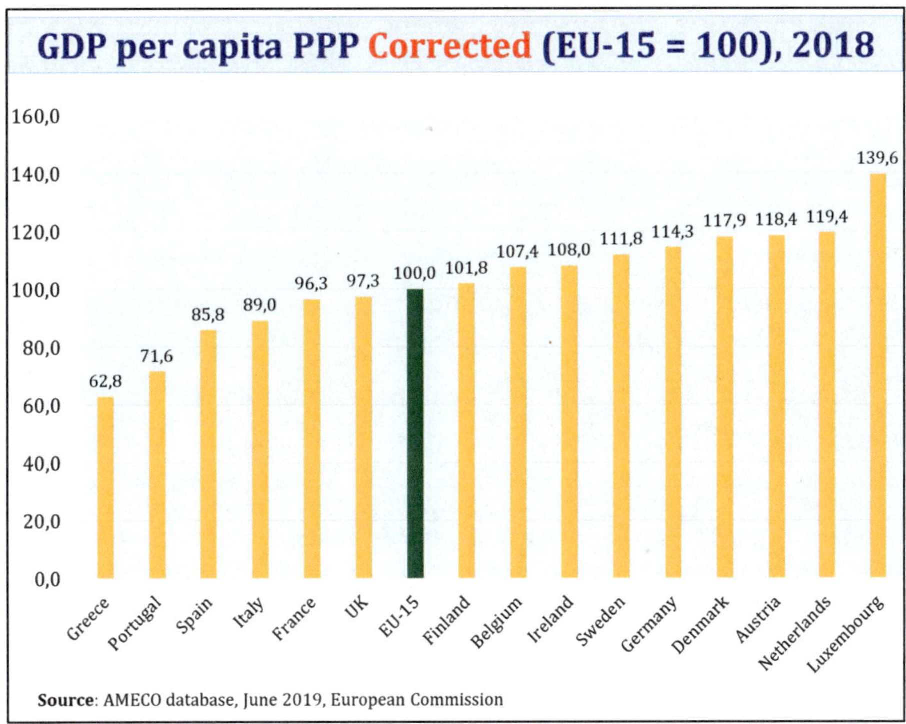

Between figures 2-1 and 2-2 there are **two** great similarities and also **two** important differences.

The *similarities* are that there is still much diversity among EU countries and that both Greece and Portugal remain the poorest ones.

The two significant *differences* respect the right side of the figure. First Ireland is no longer the second wealthiest EU country, but the seventh, and Luxembourg is now "only" ± 40% (39,6) above the average and not ±133% as in figure 2-1.

What is going on?

Let's start with **Luxembourg**, a central and small country (with ± half a million inhabitants), where 40% of its workforce daily crosses its borders, coming from France, Germany and Belgium.

They work in Luxembourg. And thus the wealth that they produce must be taken into account when calculating the gross domestic product. But they are not residents and so they cannot be considered for the per capita value. They appear in the numerator, but not in the denominator of the GDP per capita quotient (domestic income divided by domestic residents), as GDP per capita is the wealth created in a country divided by its inhabitants, the <u>residents</u>.

And so, the result is that Luxembourg's income per capita is almost **70%** inflated (232,6 in figure 2-1 divided by 139,6 in figure 2-2).

Why doesn't the EU central statistical office correct that? Because it shouldn't. The concept at the core of the GDP per capita is the income produced *within* the borders of a country divided by its residents. As ± 40% "run away" every evening to their homes in Germany, France, etc., they are not residents, and so cannot be accounted for in the GDP per capita.

Is that correct? It is. Does that make sense? No. And that **is why one should not use GDP to measure income.**

Let us now turn to the case of **Ireland** which in figure 2-1 is the *second* and in figure 2-2 the *seventh* wealthiest European country. Again, what's going on? Why the difference?

Ireland has one of the world lowest corporate tax rates[1] and so many multinationals (Apple, Google, Microsoft, Facebook, Dell, etc.) use internal accounting to transfer profits to artificially created headquarters or subsidiaries in Ireland. Although they benefit from lower taxation, in reality these multinationals have **no** operations in Ireland, whatsoever.

But the transferred profits appear (and must so) in the GDP and their amount is quite significant since ± 70% of the world trade is in the hands of multinationals.

Those profits 1) enter into Ireland, 2) are accounted for in the gross **domestic** (internal) product, and then 3) after being (slightly) taxed, 4) are immediately "exported" as dividends.[2]

To account for this, the Irish statistical office[3] reduces the national income by taking out the retained profits of multinationals artificially headquartered but with no real operations in Ireland, as well as the depreciation of intellectual property which belongs to foreigners. That **modified national income** is the statistic in figure 2-2 regarding Ireland, as profits from "box office multinationals", be they immediately or later repatriated, are merely accounting money which enters, stays for a while, pays a little tax and leaves sooner, rather than later back to their legitimate foreign owners.

And so to evaluate the **real** standard of living of the Irish that factor must be corrected. The amount varies naturally from year to

---

[1] Theoretically a tax rate of only 12,5% on profits, but in practice far lower due to many deductions and exemptions.

[2] Part of the profits may remain for a while as retained earnings but sooner, or later will be sent back to the foreign owners.

[3] Other national statistics offices such as Luxembourg's stick to the GDP, as they benefit from an enhanced image due to inflated numbers.

year depending on the in and out flows of "transferred profits", but in 2018 (the year of both figures 2-1 and 2-2) the required correction value was ± 38%. And here, again, the European central statistical office cannot change the gross domestic product evaluation of Ireland, since GDP corresponds to the wealth formally registered <u>within</u> the geographic boundaries of Ireland.

The best way to avoid the anomalies which the examples of **Luxembourg** and **Ireland** illustrate is to replace **GDP** by the **national income**, which as its name indicates is the income earned by **nationals** only, discounting those of foreigners, be they multinationals (as in the case of Ireland), or daily migrants (as happens with Luxembourg).

However, while **national income** is the statistic generally used by the World Bank, it is an exception to most other world institutions and economists which still use the GDP. At the core of their difference is the focus on *geography* or *nationals*. And so to change from the former to the latter one takes into account all types of monetary transfers, salaries due to <u>i</u>mmigrants or <u>e</u>migrants, interests, profits, rents, which cross countries borders.

And that is why national income is such a better statistic than domestic product to measure the standard of living of a population: after accounting for what is produced and manufactured in a geographical area, nationals live only with whatever monetary value remains inside.

And given the increasing globalization and liberalization of the in and out flows of both people and money (in top of goods, that is exports - imports), the trend is for an ever greater difference between the two statistics.

Luxembourg and **Ireland** are extreme examples. But there are many others. **Portugal** as mentioned before, went bankrupt in the beginning of this decade, although in terms of GDP per capita it had been converging fast with the EU average. The Portuguese economy seemed to be moving ahead. There was no warning. No signal of alarm, based on GDP figures.

Nevertheless quite a different picture in terms of national income due to the interest paid to foreigners on an increasing national debt: in the five years before the crisis, the real evolution of the economy (measured by national income per capita) was less than **1/5 (only 17%)** of that indicated by GDP per capita.

Conclusion

No statistic is to be expected to be perfect in an imperfect world. And so, it makes no sense to give up on a candle when there is no electricity.

But that is not the issue. The issue is that, before, in order to compare standards of living, **GDP** did a "reasonable job" in the past. Nowadays however, with the increasing financial flows and movement of people, **national income** is incomparably better. Although many fail to realize that and act accordingly.

And to *measure adequately is the first step into manage well.*

Fine. So the best way to measure the standard of living is through the national income, not the GDP. But how to increase it?

Here, many economists not only point out the advantages of economic blocks (European Union, Mercosur, etc.), but also that they contribute to greater cohesion, convergence, similarity, among the member countries income.

However, the next chapter shows that that is not the case.

On the contrary, within economic blocks (such as the European Union) countries standards of living tend to become **increasingly different**. Countries **diverge**. In spite of the money that the wealthier taxpayers send to the poorer ones.

2.2
Within Economic Blocks, Countries (And Federal States) Tend to Diverge (Not to Converge)

Proximity and similarity are
two *different* things.

(-)

There is nowadays a trend toward the **liberalization** of global trade. Indeed, in **spite of recent reversals** (in the transpacific trade agreement) and some tariffs wars (between the USA and China), the world is today, generally speaking, a freer economic space than a few decades ago.

First, due to the decrease of all types of trade barriers (tariffs, quotas, customs inspections, etc.) under the auspices of the *World Trade Organization.*

And then given the formation of economic blocks all over the world, being the most important the ASEAN (Association of Southeast Asian Nations), the Mercosur, NAFTA and the European Union[1].

The advantages are lower prices of goods due to the disappearance of 1) trade barriers, 2) greater specialization where countries have competitive advantages and the benefits of a larger market in creating 3) economies of scale and 4) experience effects (learning curve).

Then, in the special case of economic blocks there are additional advantages: free movement of labor and capital, central policies

---

[1] Other examples are the Commonwealth of Independent States (created by the republics of the former Soviet Union), the Economic Community of West African States (ECOWAS) and the Southern African Development Community (SADC).

common to all member countries and financing from wealthier to poorer countries.

It is thus to be expected that within economic unions, there is not only a general increase in welfare, but also an economic convergence, that is, greater income similarity, among its members. After all it is easier to copy than to innovate, regardless if innovations are of product or process. Whatever.

In short, central financing and the spread of innovations should bring greater similarity of standards of living for all within an economic block.

It makes sense. Only that… **it is not true**. The empirical evidence is that within economic unions the trend is toward an ever greater difference among standards of living. Toward divergence. The richer become richer. And the poorer, poorer. In relative terms.

That is the conclusion in figure 2-3 (where the analysis is done for the last quarter of century with the most recent data available)[1].

---

[1]The analysis is done for EU-15 and not the Eurozone or EU-28 as the former is older and thus allows for a longer term analysis. Besides it should be used national income instead of GDP. However there is no national income data for the federal states of the USA. Thus, to assure comparability GDP is used, as second best.

Comparison of the income of top and bottom four EU-15 countries and USA states

Countries/ States	EU-15		USA	
	1995	**2018**	**1997**	**2018**
Top four countries/states (descending GDP per capita PPS)	Luxembourg	Luxembourg	District of Columbia	District of Columbia
	Germany	Ireland	Delaware	New York
	Austria	Netherlands	Connecticut	Massachusetts
	Netherlands	Austria	Alaska	Delaware
Bottom four countries/states (descending GDP per capita PPS)	Ireland	Italy	Arkansas	Idaho
	Spain	Spain	Montana	West Virginia
	Greece	Portugal	West Virginia	Arkansas
	Portugal	Greece	Mississippi	Mississippi
Top / Bottom ratio	1,7	2,08	2,59	2,66
Differences in membership within ◯ and % of difference	+22%		+2,7%	

Note: For the USA the data is for 1997 instead of 1995.
Sources: USA: US Bureau of Economic Analysis, 2019; EU-15: AMECO, August 2019

In 1995 the wealthiest **four** European countries (Netherlands, Austria, Germany and Luxembourg), had in average more 70% of income than the poorer four: Portugal, Greece, Spain and Ireland (ratio **of 1,7**).

In 2018, however, the top four had more than double the income of the poorer ones (+108%)[1]: ratio **of 2,08**. Thus, the difference in

---

[1] Between 1995 and 2018 in the group of the richer countries there was a single change (Germany was replaced by Ireland). In the group of the poorer countries there was also only one modification: Ireland was replaced by Italy.

income from richer and poorer countries increased relatively by almost a quarter (22%: 2,08/1,7).

What about if we compare the **seven** (top) and seven (bottom), as per figure 2-4?

Figure 2-4

Comparison of the income of top and bottom seven EU-15 countries and USA states

Countries/States	EU-15		USA	
	1995	2018	1997	2018
Top seven countries/states (descending GDP per capita PPS)	Luxembourg	Luxembourg	District of Columbia	District of Columbia
	Germany	Ireland	Delaware	New York
	Austria	Netherlands	Connecticut	Massachusetts
	Netherlands	Austria	Alaska	Delaware
	Sweden	Denmark	New York	Connecticut
	Denmark	Germany	Massachusetts	California
	Belgium	Sweden	New Jersey	Washington
Bottom seven countries/states (descending GDP per capita PPS)	France	Finland	Idaho	Montana
	United Kingdom	United Kingdom	Alabama	South Carolina
	Finland	France	Oklahoma	Alabama
	Ireland	Italy	Arkansas	Idaho
	Spain	Spain	Montana	West Virginia
	Greece	Portugal	West Virginia	Arkansas
	Portugal	Greece	Mississippi	Mississippi
Top / Bottom ratio	1,42	1,65	2,15	2,21
Differences in membership within ⬭ and % of difference	+16%		+2,8%	

Note: For the USA the data is for 1997 instead of 1995.
Sources: USA: US Bureau of Economic Analysis, 2019; EU-15: AMECO, August 2019

In 1995 the EU-15 difference in average wealth was 42% (ratio **of 1,42**) and in 2018 it increased to 65% (ratio **of 1,65**)[1]. Again there was divergence.

And if we compare **all** (15) countries within EU-15? For such a purpose economists use a statistic called the **Gini index** which varies from zero (all countries have equal income) to one (meaning that theoretically one country would have all the income and all others zero income). So the higher the value, the greater the diversity in countries income.

In 1995 the value of the EU-15 Gini index was 0,156 but in 2018 it had become 0,195 (an increase of 25%: 0,195 / 0,156).

In short, in roughly a quarter of a century income **disparity among European countries increased considerably**.

But, is that something peculiar, **unique**, to the European Union?

The answer is **no**, since again the **Gini index** between 1995 and 2018 of the federal states of **USA** (a two centuries old economic

---

[1] In 1995 the top seven were (by decreasing order of wealth) Luxembourg, Germany, Austria, Netherlands, Sweden, Denmark and Belgium; and the bottom seven were France, United Kingdom, Finland, Ireland, Spain, Greece and the poorest of all, Portugal. In 2018 the top seven were Luxembourg, Ireland, Netherlands, Austria, Denmark, Germany and Sweden; and at the bottom there were Finland, UK, France, Italy, Spain, Portugal and Greece.

So the major changes in a quarter of century were: Ireland shifted from the bottom to the top group, while Belgium, now the 8th wealthier country, left the top seven group. Everything else remained the same.

At the bottom Portugal and Greece changed places as the poorest country and Ireland was replaced by Italy.

Today the poorer countries are the five often called Club Mediterranee (Greece, Portugal, Spain, Italy and France) then the UK and Finland.

union) also increased from **0,163** to **0,211**, almost a 30% increase (figure 2-5).

Figure 2-5

Comparing the Gini Index

(for all EU-15 countries and states of the USA)

Block / Year		EU-15	USA
1995		0,156	0,163
2018		0,195	0,211
Increase	Absolute	+0,039	+0,048
	% (2018 / 1995)	+25%	+29%

Notes:

    1) Gini Index: 0 – Minimum; 1 – Maximum

    2) For the USA the data is for 1997 instead of 1995.

Source: AMECO, June 2019, European Commission; US Bureau of Economic Analysis, 2019. Latest data available.

And (as per figures 2-3 and 2-4 before) if we compare the top and bottom **four**, the difference in income also increased from +159% to +166%, as if we put the top **seven** against the bottom seven, the numbers are 115% and 121%, for 1997 and 2018 respectively, a percentual increase of +6%.

Still if we compare the top **ten** and bottom ten the difference increased from +92% to +99%[1].

------

[1] In the case of EU-15 one could obviously compare only seven to seven.

In short, both within the European Union and the USA, and regardless if we compare groups of four, groups of seven, groups of ten, or all countries (or federal states) together (with the Gini index), the outcome is the same: with time, diversity in income increases. The gap between the richer and the poorer augments. The trend is toward **divergence**, not convergence.

That is still reinforced if we compare the European Union against the USA: as per figure 2-5, the Gini indexes of the **USA** (both in 1995 and 2018) are **greater** than those of Europe (0,163 against 0,156 and 0,211 against 0,195, respectively).

Since the USA is a centuries old economic union and Europe only decades so, that confirms that with time the trend is toward divergence, not convergence. Diversity, not similarity. And in spite that the central USA budget is far greater than that of the European Union.

But, **why** is there such a trend? After all the arguments for convergence referred at the beginning of this chapter seem quite compelling: easier to copy than to innovate; and central governments sending funds available to poorer regions to improve their competitiveness.

The answer regards the strong advantages of wealthier countries and federal states. **First** to labor: better wages attract the best; there is a brain drain of the poorer regions.[1]

Second, being the richer, more dynamic regions, also offer greater opportunities to remunerate well the capital.

---

[1] Really not only a brain but also an "arms" drain: those with more initiative, hardworking, less risk averse, etc. are generally those who migrate. Those who lack that, stay behind. As with all general rules, it allows for exceptions.

Entrepreneurship means shifting resources from lower value to higher value opportunities. Something quite easy within economic blocks where there are few if any internal barriers of labor and capital movements.

Conclusion

Within economic blocks there is a trend toward **divergence**. And empirical evidence for that comes from **three** sources.

When we analyze the **EU-15 over time**: be it the top four against bottom four; or the top seven against bottom seven; or still the Gini index (all fifteen countries).

Then, the same conclusion is reached when we analyze the evolution of the federal states of the **USA**: again in terms of groups of four, seven, ten and all states (Gini index).

And finally when we make not longitudinal, but a **geographic** comparison between the "older" USA and the most recent European Union.

Two words of caution are due, here. First, divergence should not be confused with impoverishment, since the fact that the poorer countries become poorer **relatively**, does not mean that they also become so in **absolute** terms. Only that the poorer **improved less** than the richer.

And second, still a different question is if the poorer countries would have been better off if they did not belong to an economic union?

That is a difficult question to answer as we do not have parallel worlds (with e.g. Greece between 1995 and 2018 simultaneously belonging to and not belonging to the European Union).

And if we were to compare the 25 years before (e.g.) Greece joined the European Union with the 25 years thereafter, we could be comparing "oranges and apples" as the periods are not similar. The world from 1970 to 1995 was quite a different place from that from 1995 to 2018. For instance, in the early seventies Greece was under a dictatorship (as was the case with Portugal and Spain).

Anyway, the answer—given the advantages of trade liberalization in general and economic unions in particular—is probably not. It pays off to be a member of the EU, ASEAN, NAFTA, etc.

That does not mean however that all (e.g. EU) policies are necessarily positive.

For instance, **central financing** from the richer to the poorer countries (regions) is an advantage, or a handicap? Again, what is the empirical evidence? Do the numbers suggest that there is at least some room for **doubt?**

Let's turn to the next chapter.

2.3
Financing Poorer Countries Leads Them to Fall Behind?

What you incentivize is what you get.

Jack Welch (former GE CEO)

In the European Union whose central budget is a small fraction (3,63%) of that of the USA[1], there are **four** major types of **central funds**: ERDF, ESF, EAFRD, and EMFF which all countries can benefit from. They focus on several areas: agriculture, the fishing industry, human capital, etc.

And there is a **fifth one** called the **cohesion fund** *aimed at Member States whose Gross National Income (GNI) per inhabitant is less than 90% of the EU average. It aims to reduce economic and social disparities and to promote sustainable development* (quote)[2]. In short its aim is **to promote convergence through sustainable development**.

During the last quarter of century, as per figure 2-6 and by decreasing amount, there were four EU-15 recipients: Spain, Greece, Portugal and Ireland[3].

---

[1] The same questions raised in this chapter (which for the sake of simplicity focus solely on the European Union), can also be raised regarding the USA and other economic unions, as well.

[2] Source: European Commission:
 https://ec.europa.eu/regional policy/en/funding/cohesion-fund

[3] Other countries also benefited from the cohesion fund namely: Bulgaria, Croatia, Cyprus, Czech Republic, Estonia, Hungary, Latvia, Lithuania, Malta, Poland, Romania, Slovakia and Slovenia.
However, just as in the previous chapter, one will focus on the EU-15, to allow for a longer period of analysis.

During that period the four countries received almost fifty billion euros: Spain ± **25**, Greece ± **11**, Portugal **10,1** and Ireland **2,125**.

Figure 2-6

Cohesion funds	
Countries	Total amount in the period (1994-2019) – in million euros
Spain	24.470
Greece	10.560
Portugal	10.089
Ireland	2.125
Total	47.244

Notes:

1) Value received until the 20th of August 2019.

2) Spain and Ireland received the last payment from cohesion funds in 2015.

Source: European Commission

And, what were the **results**? Let's divide the answer in three parts: 1) **growth**; 2) economic **competitiveness**; 3) and **other variables**: *transparency* and *economic freedom*.

Growth

Figure 2-7 shows two lines. In **blue** is, for each country, the percentage that the amount of cohesion funds represented in national income.[1]

And the **red** line is the yearly growth rate[2] of national income in the period.

---

[1] For the period 1994-2019: $\dfrac{\text{Average amount received in cohesion funds}}{\text{Average national income}}$

[2] Average compound.

As can be seen they are almost inversely related, countries where the cohesion funds represented a larger percentage of the national income, grew less; and vice-versa.

Figure 2-7

Period 1994-2019: Comparing growth rate with % of cohesion funds in national income

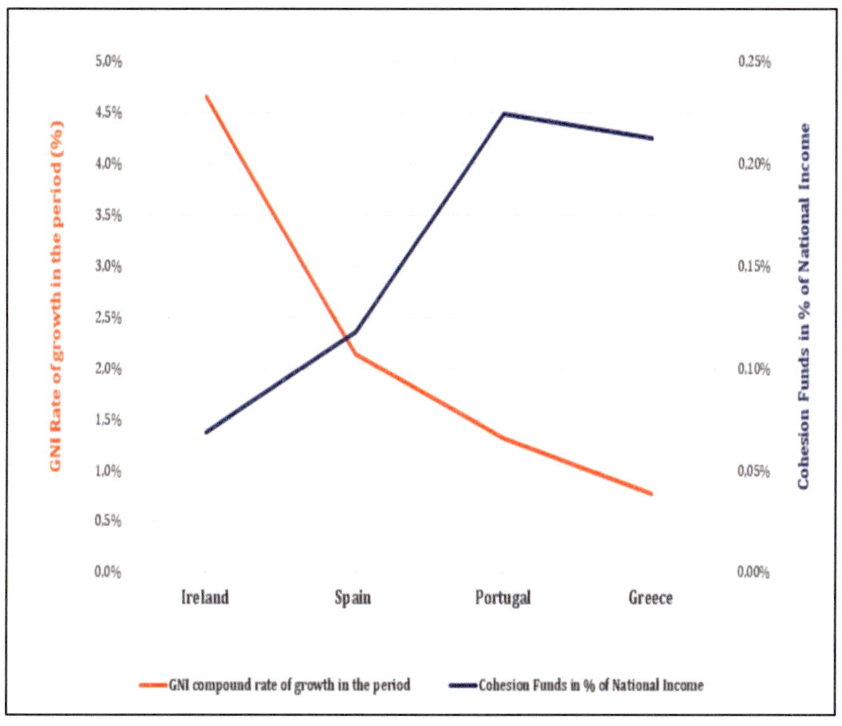

Notes:

1) Value received until the 20th of August 2019.

2) Spain and Ireland received the last payment from cohesion funds in 2015. Therefore, to calculate the average amount received per year both for Spain and Ireland, one considered 22 years instead of 26. The same is done for the gross national income: only the years from 1994 until 2015 were considered for the average national income and the annual growth rate.

3) Gross National Income at constant prices.

Source: European Commission

Then, figure 2-8 compares the income of each country in the beginning and at the end of the quarter of a century: in 1994 all countries were below 80% of the EU-15 average and in 2019 Ireland is the only one above average (almost 10%).

The others remain below: Spain at 85% of the EU-15 average (it converged ± 8%)[1], Portugal about the same (converged 1,5%)[2] and Greece diverged (from 75,5% to 63,3% of the EU-15 average)!

Figure 2-8
GNI per capita PPS, EU-15 = 100

Country	1994	2019	Difference 2019-1994
Ireland	78,9	108,4 [1]	+29,5
Greece	75,5	63,3	-12,2
Spain	76,6	84,5	+7,9
Portugal	68,9	70,4	+1,5

Note:

(1) Ireland GNI corrected equals $\frac{total\ GNI\ corrected}{total\ GNI} \times GNI\ per\ capita\ PPS\ (EU - 15 = 100)$. The formula differs from the one used in chapter 2.1, since in this case we are comparing Irish GNI per capita with the GNI per capita average of the EU-15, and not with the average of the GDP per capita.
Source: AMECO, May 2020.

Four aspects are noteworthy regarding these figures: 1) a **no surprise**; then 2) **two surprises**; and finally 3) a **word of caution**.

The **no surprise** is that the poorer countries in 1994, Portugal, Greece and Spain (see figure 2-8) received every year a larger

---

[1] 84,5-76,6

[2] 70,4-68,9

amount of cohesion funds than the richer ones: both in total amount (figure 2-6) and percentage of national income (blue line in figure 2-7).

That is nothing but natural. As the purpose of the cohesion funds is to promote competitiveness, they should go to those countries which were more behind.

However what comes as a **real surprise** is that those countries which received more cohesion funds **grew less** than those which received less cohesion funds.

Indeed, there is an inverse relation regardless if one accounts for the cohesion funds in percentage of national income (figure 2-7).

In other words, that the poorer received more, fine. That poorer, in spite of receiving more, grew less, that's surprising.

Not to mention (**second surprise**) that during a quarter of a century, Portugal converged almost nothing with the EU average (only 1,5% per figure 2-8) and Greece diverged more than 12% (from 75,5 to 63,3% in figure 2-8).

Finally, a **word of caution**: no causation is suggested here, as there are two ways to read the data.

The first is that countries performing worse, received more: that corresponds to *putting (more) money into a problem.*

And the other is that *those countries which receive more... (tend to) grow less.*

Both conclusions are possible. And together with still a third, namely that there is no causation whatsoever, but a simple association between growth and cohesion funds. A mere *coincidence*, being both variables consequences of a third common cause, whatever that may be.

But whatever the interpretation, it cannot escape a word: **disappointment**.

Indeed another way of seeing how much disappointment the results are is to compare how much each year a country received in funding and how much its economy **grew**: year after year.

After all, national income is the sum of all salaries and other factors of remuneration.

And so, if (e.g.) the income is 100 and the value of funding received is 2, income should at the end of the year be 102. Not accounting for the Keynesian effect to be discussed in the next chapter.[1]

Let's take Portugal as an example and figure 2-9 shows how much in this millennium Portugal received in EU financing in percentage of national income (in red) and how much its income grew (in **blue**), every single year.

---

[1] Basically, if I receive 100 and my saving rate is 10%, I spend 90% increasing the income of others by 90 (90% x 100 = 90); and then by the same token third parties income is augmented by 0,9 x 90 = 81, and so on; thus increasing overall national income by 100 + 90 + 81 + etc. = 271, etc.

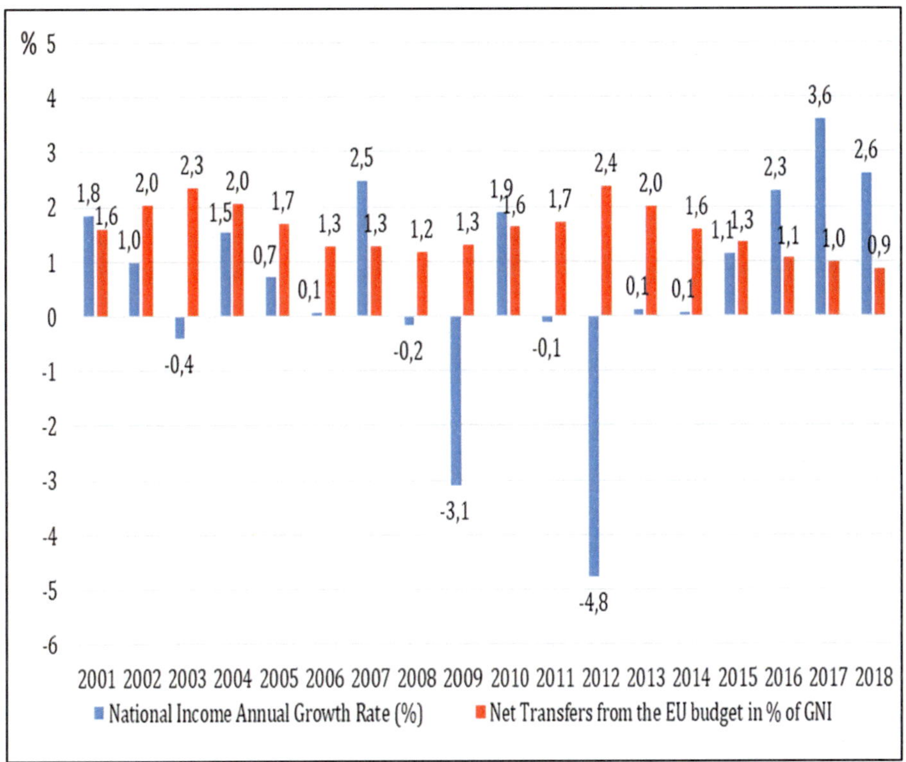

Sources: Ameco, February 2020; Pordata, July 2019. Most recent data available.

Note: 1) Annual growth rate of Gross National Income at constant prices.

2) Net transfers = Public transfers from the EU minus Public payments to the EU

3) Public transfers received from the EU include the five Structural and Investment Funds, refunds and other receipts provided for in the EU budget. The five funds are: European regional development fund (ERDF), European social fund (ESF), Cohesion fund (CF), European agricultural fund for rural development (EAFRD) and European maritime and fisheries fund (EMFF).

As can be seen in twelve of the eighteen years (2/3), Portuguese national income grew less than the country received in EU funding:

the first year 2001 was an exception, but 2002, 2003, 2004, 2005, 2006, etc. were the rule.

However one should note that here, we are not speaking only of cohesion funds but of all five types together: 1) European regional development fund (ERDF), 2) European social fund (ESF), 3) Cohesion fund (CF), 4) European agricultural fund for rural development (EAFRD) and 5) European maritime and fisheries fund (EMFF).

Economic competitiveness

Let us now detail the analysis by looking at the economic performance of these countries in terms of several indexes, starting with **competitiveness**, measured by an index developed by the *Institute for Management Development*.

Figure 2-10 leads us to two main conclusions (always regarding the last quarter of century):

First, Spain, Portugal and Greece, all **worsened** in terms of their competitiveness ranking: Spain went from 26th to 36th in the world; Portugal from 32nd to 39th; and Greece from 36th to 58th.

Second, the **exception** is Ireland which improved from 10th to 7th, being Ireland precisely among all four countries the one which received less funding (as per figures 2-6 and 2-7): ± 20% of Portugal's and Greece's amounts and less than 9% that of Spain.[1]

---

[1] However both Ireland and Spain stopped.

Figure 2-10

Competitiveness world ranking

Years / Countries	1995	2019	Difference [1]
Spain	26th	36th	**+10**
Greece	36th	58th	**+22**
Portugal	32nd	39th	**+7**
Ireland	10th	7th	**-3**

Source: International Management Development, consulted in August 2019

Note: [1] A negative number represents an improvement in competitiveness and a positive one a worsening.

Thus, cohesion funds failed to improve the competitiveness ranking of the recipients with the single exception of Ireland, precisely the country which benefited less from those funds.[1]

---

[1] There are two reasons why it is better to use the ranking than the rating (the absolute grade which varies from 0—bad to 100—excellent) also supplied by the Institute for Management Development:

First: the ranking provides for comparison, while the rating, being absolute values, do not account for the overall evolution of all countries over time, either inflation or deflation.

Second: a potential disadvantage of using the ranking could however be, that the number of countries analyzed has increased: indeed in 1995 there were 47 countries analyzed and in 2019, 63 countries. However the majority of the new 16 countries which were included in the analysis do not belong to the first world, to the OECD group. Those 16 countries are: Bulgaria, Croatia, Cyprus, Kazakhstan, Latvia, Lithuania, Mongolia, Peru, Qatar, Romania, Saudi Arabia, Slovak Republic, Slovenia, Turkey, UAE and Ukraine. Of these, only five (Latvia, Lithuania, Slovak Republic, Slovenia and Turkey) are part of the OECD.

In any case, even if one takes into account the increase of new countries analyzed and thus one divides each country's ranking by the total number of countries analyzed, thus creating a ratio whose value the lower, the better (lower ranking

How is that possible?

The only explanation is that *in spite* of the advantages of belonging to the largest economic union (as analyzed in the previous chapter: economies of scale, specialization effects, etc.) and in spite of the considerable funding received, there must be some factors working **against** the progress of the countries beneficiaries of the cohesion funds.

Other variables: economic freedom and transparency

Heritage Foundation (in Washington) and Transparency International (in Berlin) are two NGOs which produce worldwide rankings in terms of **economic freedom** and **transparency**, respectively. What happened to the rankings of the **four** countries in terms of these variables, **economic freedom and transparency?**

As per figure 2-11, in general their ranking worsened with again the single exception of **Ireland**. And **only** regarding economic freedom, but not transparency.[1]

Indeed **Spain** worsened 4 positions in transparency and 23 in economic freedom; **Greece** 30 in transparency and 64 (!) in economic freedom; **Portugal** 8 in transparency and 24 (!) in

near the top in the numerator and greater total number of countries analyzed in the denominator), the conclusion is that from 1995 to 2019 Portugal ratio improved only slightly (from 0,68 in 1995 to 0,62 in 2019), that of Spain remained basically constant (0,55 and 0,57) and that of Greece worsened (from 0,77 to 0,92).

[1] Once more note that the number of countries analyzed increased in transparency (from 41 in 1995 to 180 in 2019) and in economic freedom (from 101 in 1995 to 180 in 2019). However in the first year of analysis there were already and respectively 41 and 101 countries analyzed covering the OECD countries, with whom European countries should be compared to, and not with third world ones.

economic freedom; finally **Ireland's** ranking decreased 7 in transparency but (the single exception in eight) improved 14 in economic freedom.

Figure 2-11

Countries by order of funds received	Transparency ranking		Economic freedom	
	1995	2019	1995	2019
Spain	26th	30th	34th	57th
Greece	30th	60th	42nd	106th
Portugal	22nd	30th	38th	62nd
Ireland	11th	18th	20th	6th

Sources: Transparency International – Corruption Perceptions Index, consulted February 2020; Heritage Foundation – Economic freedom index, consulted February 2020

Why is **transparency** important?

Because its opposite, corruption is, as Nobel laureate Milton Friedman put it, a *tax on economic development*.

Resources are scarce. Their allocation must thus be optimized, meaning being used by firms which are most productive, in terms of quality, quantity and time.

Corruption prevents that. It allocates resources suboptimally to less competitive firms.

And then **economic freedom**, market liberty, means that there is a lot of competitors in each industry.

With few monopolies and oligopolies, the consumer is sovereign and free to choose. Just as in "political markets" with the vote, citizens can now select among many firms where to place the money.

Two things follow. First, the less competitive companies are *"pushed"* out of the market. Second, all firms are *"pulled"* to improve their performance. Every single day. In order to survive and have profits. Thus, as has been said, **a competitor is a helper** (Edmund Burke).

So, it should come as no surprise that there is a strong (co)relation among transparency, economic freedom and competitiveness.[1]

Figure 2-12 indicates the **correlation coefficients** between economic competitiveness and economic freedom: **0,74** and **0,77** for ranking (ordinal values) and within brackets for rating (cardinal, absolute values).

As it is known the correlation coefficients vary between -1 (negative association meaning that when one variable increases the other variable decreases by the same percentage), to +1 (perfect association, that is both variables vary in the same sense and percentage) and with the value of zero indicating that there is no association whatsoever.

So the fact that both values are positive and close to one means that the variables (*economic freedom* and *economic competitiveness*) are **strongly associated.**

---

[1] Measured by an index such as that of the Institute for Management Development.

The same happens between *transparency* and *economic competitiveness* (correlation of 0,72 and 0,72) and between *economic freedom* and *transparency* (correlation of 0,69 and 0,71): economic freedom means strong competition in the markets, thus few monopolies, less firms with great market power and as it is known, *if power corrupts, absolute power corrupts absolutely* (Lord Acton).

Finally one should note that all correlation coefficients in figure 2-12 are statistically significant at zero level, meaning that the probability that their value (their positive association) is due to mere chance is… null, zero—see figure 2-12.

Figure 2-12

The correlation between transparency, economic freedom and competitiveness

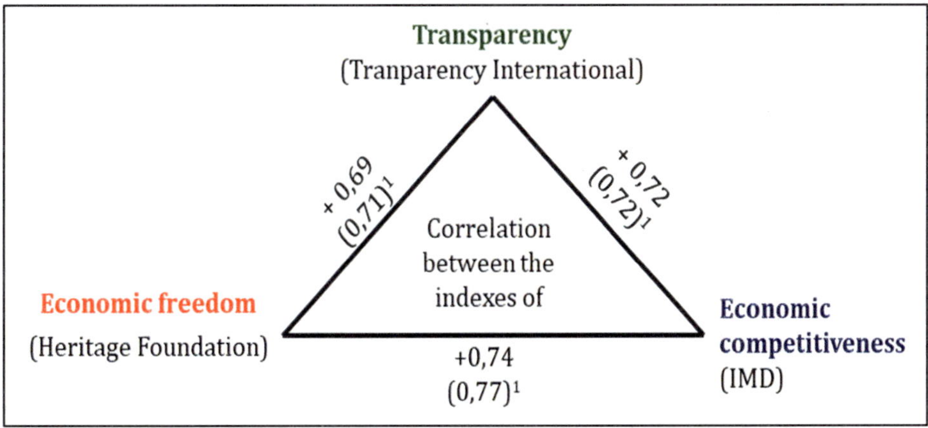

Notes: Correlation among the first 55 countries of the economic freedom index.
[1] Correlation coefficients: Spearman and within brackets the Pearson coefficient

The fact that the three variables are associated[1] means that they can constitute a **virtuous** circle (in this case a virtuous triangle):

---

[1] Again such an association does not mean causality. In this case it can be argued that the stronger causality is from transparency and economic freedom **to** economic

when one of the variables improves, it causes the others to move in the same sense; or a **vicious** circle (triangle): when one variable worsens, it brings the others downward too.

In the case of Greece, Portugal, Spain and Ireland, as they received funds to increase their competitiveness, that did not happen. On the contrary. Just like transparency and economic freedom.[1]

Conclusion

What do the numbers indicate regarding the four EU-15 countries which benefited from cohesion funds to improve their competitiveness? What was the result? **Six things.**

First: regarding three countries, Greece **diverged**, Portugal basically did not converge and Spain converged slightly (see figure 2-9).[2]

---

competitiveness. However it can also be reasoned that in most competitive countries, as people are richer… temptations are…lower.

[1] Ireland is the exception. Regarding economic freedom and competitiveness but not transparency (see figures 2-10 and 2-11).

[2] In real euros. In percentage of the European Union, Spain, Portugal and Greece improved. But in real terms not. The reason being that in order to improve in real terms (in euros), it is not enough to grow more than he EU average, but one needs also to grow sufficiently more to offset the initial difference. As an example, let's say that a country's income per capita is, at the beginning of a period only (e.g.) 2/3 (66%) of the EU average (100); then if the country grows two percent and Europe in average grows by 1,5% at the end of the period the country improved 2 x 66% = 1,32 euros, but the average augmented 1,5 x 100 = 1,5 euros, which is obviously higher.

So, in order to decrease the absolute difference in terms of acquisition power ("money in the pocket") a country that at the beginning of the period has an income of only 66% of the average must grow at a rate (%) which is $\frac{100}{66}$ = 1,5 higher that of the average.

If the average of countries grow 2%, the country must grow 1,5 times more: 1,5 x 2% = 3%.

If the average grows 3% the country must grow at 1,5 x 3% = 4,5%. And so on.

Second: the one which converged (Ireland) is precisely the one which received by far **less** funding (see figures 2-6 and 2-7).

Third: in the one country analyzed (Portugal) national income **grew**, in general, year after year, less than the amount of financing it received. From all five types of funds.

Fourth: in general, countries worsened in the **competitiveness** of their economy.

Fifth: and also in terms of the ranking of **transparency**.

And **sixth** (and finally): again also in **economic freedom**.

Is there a way to improve that? Most probably exerting greater **control** regarding how funds are used. **After all what happens is not what one expects, but what one inspects.**

And what is a single word to sum it all up?: **disappointment.** At the very least the results of EU funding are disappointing. Even because there seems to be no **Keynesian effect**. Or is there? And should there be? Let's turn to the next chapter.

2.4
Keynesianism Is
(Increasingly) Irrelevant

In the long term, we are all dead.

John Maynard Keynes

2.4.1 Introduction

John Maynard Keynes, the most well-known economist of the 20th century, proposed a new approach to economy policy based on **ten main items**.

First: frequently economies are working under high *unemployment* and underutilization of other resources: factories and machinery.

Second: economies can stay *for long* in such a situation, without any natural trend to improve (economists say that there is an *equilibrium*, no tendency to change).

Third: why?: Because the *demand* for goods and services is not enough ("to put the economy back to work").

Thus (**fourth**): the solution is to *increase demand*.

Fifth: how? The government should augment its *investment* (with programs to build roads, and all types of infrastructures)[1] and that will produce a greater than proportional increase in income.

---

[1] And here Keynesianism differs from another economics schools which defend the increase in money supply.

Sixth: why? Let's say (e.g.) that the government starts a *public program* of new highways. That means that 1) machineries will be bought and 2) more people will be put to work.

The former will induce an increase in the production of *machinery* factories which will then buy more components and spare parts from their suppliers and these on their turn will also acquire more from their own suppliers and so on, creating a positive *chain of increasing in wealth.*

Then (**seventh**), all along this chain, companies (plus the government initially) will *hire more workers*, who with greater income will be able to buy more *consumer goods* from supermarkets, cars, leisure, services, whatever.

So *government programs* of investment trigger two chains where wealth is successively created and passed from one stage to the other. The first chain is of *industrial goods*: road machinery, components, parts, operating supplies and maintenance and repair (lubricants, etc.).

And the second chain is of *consumer goods*: clothing, food, furniture, housing, cars, leisure and so on.

Eighth: after a few stages, both the industrial and consumer chains become interconnected and mutually *reinforcing.*

Ninth: that positive momentum of wealth creating (economists call it the **Keynesian multiplier**) will not last forever but eventually *stop.*

Indeed, as one goes from stage to stage, the income created decreases slightly for two reasons: first, part of the money is not spent but *saved*, staying in banks; and second, even part of the money spent does not benefit the economy internally, but goes abroad to pay for *imports*.

So both savings and imports decrease the wealth created at each stage, after the initial impulse created by the government work programs.

Tenth: where does the money come from? Either from *debt* (borrowed by the government internally or from foreigners), or by the government's printing money, through an account created near the central bank[1].

2.4.2 The Keynesian formula

The previous ten steps are a very simple description of what economists call the **Keynesian multiplier**, whose simple formula is below with disposable income being the income families have, less the taxes they pay.

$$Keynesian\ multiplier = \cfrac{1}{\cfrac{Savings}{Disposable\ income} + \cfrac{Imports}{National\ income}}$$

And regarding this formula there are **five** worthwhile aspects:

---

[1] Besides public investment, Keynesian policies can assume other forms such as tax decreases, which augment disposable income and thus aggregate demand. We will however focus our analysis solely on the public investment effect, which is the most common policy used.

In any case, the effect of tax decreases is also limited by imports first, and (national, not governmental) borrowing if trade deficits occur.

A—The **higher** the **savings** and the higher the **imports**, the greater the first and second ratios in the denominator. Consequently the denominator increases and the whole quotient (the Keynesian multiplier) **decreases**.

B—As referred above, at every single stage of the two chains of wealth creation previously described in steps six and seven, both savings and imports, decrease the wealth created. Until the whole effect is **exhausted**.[1]

C—With the increasing trade liberalization *among* economic unions (EU, NAFTA, Mercosur, ASEAN, etc.) and even more so *within* these economic unions, the percentage of imports in national income tends to augment and thus the multiplier becomes ever smaller. That is, the Keynesian effect is wasted through the "open window" of **foreign trade**.

Which, naturally, varies from country to country. So, some have large internal markets (e.g. Brazil and the USA); in other smaller countries, trade represents a higher weight.

Indeed, as can be seen in figure 2-13, imports represent a higher percentage of national income in Ireland, Portugal and Greece than in the UK (a mid-sized country) and even less in USA (15%) and Brazil (14%).

---

[1] Frequently after two years.

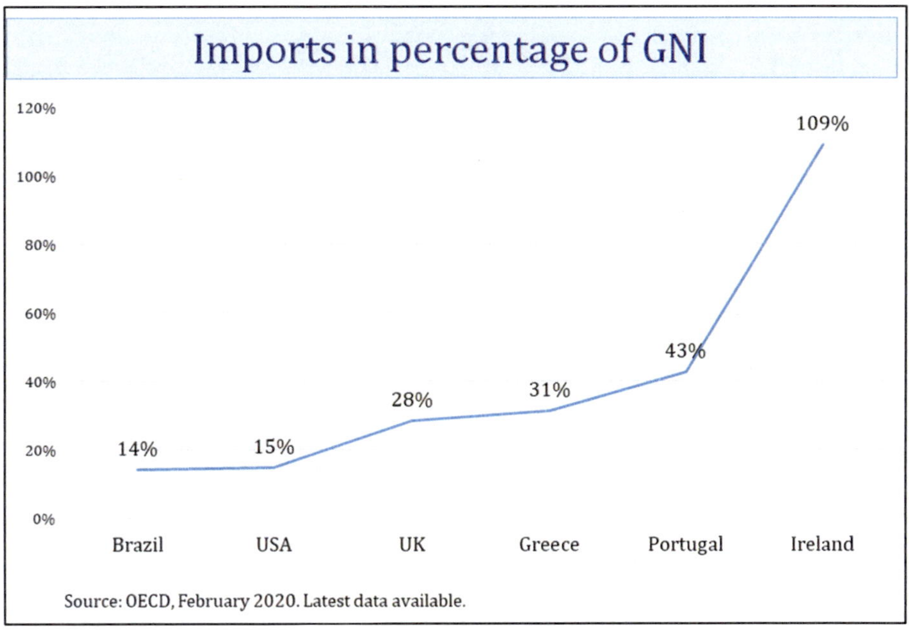

Figure 2-13

D—Keynesian programs have a greater effect on **GDP** (gross domestic product), that is wealth created in a region, than on **national income** (money which stays there); and

E—The Keynesian impact is greater when governments can **create money** (simply drawing it from an artificial account created at the central bank), than when they cannot do that because they do not issue their own currency. Or they can issue it, but its currency is not accepted as an international reserve by other countries.

Examples of countries which are monetary independent are the UK, Denmark, Norway; of countries which cannot issue currency are all Eurozone members whose monetary supply is controlled by the European central bank; and of countries whose currency is not accepted as an international reserve are Brazil and Russia: by opposition to the US dollar and to a smaller extent the Japanese yen.

2.4.3 The hypothesis

In short, the **Keynesian multiplier** tends to **decrease**:

1. In general due to trade liberalization and the consequent increase in **imports**;
2. Even more so in **small** rather than large countries, where the internal market plays a larger (and consequently imports a lesser) role;
3. Most specially in countries which **cannot issue currency** (and therefore have to use debt to finance public works programs); or
4. Whose currency is **not accepted** as an international reserve (such as the US dollar, British pound or the Japanese yen), in substitution of gold.

We have been so far speaking about public investment, but much of the above also applies to **private** (by firms) investment although less so, since private has over public investment **two advantages:**

1. They are generally **more productive** (even in exports) as private companies must survive the market test of competition; and
2. Since investments done by firms are generally smaller than public works, they have a smaller component of **imports** and more of national, regional, and even local purchases.

Anyway, in terms of public investment, the **expectation in terms of empirical evidence** is that across all countries, there is in general terms a **weak relation** between:

- the relative weight of public investment in national income; and
- the level of national income per capita.

But then, and regardless its value, the above relation, should be:

- **Maximum** in countries 1) *large*, 2) which control their *money supply* and 3) whose currency is an *international reserve* (e.g. the USA in figure 2-14);
- **Average** in countries somewhat *smaller*, but still with 1) an independent monetary policy and 2) a currency accepted as an international reserve (UK in figure 2-14); or still 3) in large countries with a very *large internal market* (and consequently lower weight of imports on national income) such as Brazil, although its currency is not an international means of payment; and finally
- **Smallest** in 1) *small* countries and 2) *without* an independent monetary policy, the case of most Eurozone countries including Portugal, Greece and Ireland.

Figure 2-14 shows that it is so: the Keynesian multiplier is minimum in a small country such as *Portugal* (**2**); average in the *UK*—medium size and monetary independence of a reserve currency—(**2,6**); and large in the *USA*—large internal market and dollar as the international reserve—(**3,61**).

The surprise is *Brazil* (largest Keynesian multiplier of all = **4,55**) due to its very low % of imports on GDP (12,1% against 15,3% in the USA).[1]

Figure 2-14

Keynesian multiplier	Internal market	Large	Small
Can issue international reserve currency			
Yes		USA 3,61	UK 2,60
No		Brazil 4,55	Portugal 2

Formula of multiplier used:
$Keynesian\ Multiplier\ for\ an\ Open\ Economy = \dfrac{1}{(MPS + MPZ)}$

Where	$MPS = gross\ saving\ rate\ of\ households =$ $\dfrac{Gross\ Savings\ of\ Households}{Adjusted\ Gross\ Disposable\ Income}$
	$MPZ = \dfrac{Imports}{GDP}$

Values	MPS	MPZ	Multiplier
USA	0,124	0,153	3,61
UK	0,066	0,318	2,60
Brazil	0,099	0,121	4,55
Portugal	0,066	0,434	2

---

[1] The % of savings is larger in the USA (12,4%) than in Brazil (9,9%).

Sources: Ameco, most recent data available, February 2020.

Instituto Brasileiro de Geografia e Estatística – Sistema de Contas Nacionais, most recent data available. Consulted on February 2020.

OECD National Accounts Statistics: National Accounts at a Glance. Most recent data available. Consulted on February 2020.

2.4.4 The tests (empirical evidence)

Let us now move to test these hypothesis starting by the simplest possible way, as per figure 2-15, which presents the value of two types of correlation coefficients (Spearman and Pearson[1]) which measure the association between:

- The % of public investment in national income; and

- The national income per capita.

The period of analysis is this millennium (from 2000 to 2018), for a sample of 41 OECD members or associated countries[2].

---

[1] The Spearman coefficient evaluates the relation between the ranking, that is, the order, 1st / 2nd / 3rd / etc. among variables and the Pearson coefficient which measures also the relation, but now in terms of absolute, cardinal values, not ordinal values.

In either cases, the correlation coefficients, vary between -1 meaning that there is an inverse, a negative, relation between the variables (when one variable increases the other decreases proportionally), and +1 in which case the association is perfect and positive: both variables move in the same sense and proportionally; when the coefficient correlation is zero that means that there is no relation whatsoever between the variables.

And below brackets is the level of statistical significance of the correlation coefficients that is the probability that its value is due to pure chance. So the lower the value the greater the significance of the correlation. The interval of the value is between zero (no probability of being due to chance) and one (absolutely sure "it… just happened").

[2] The OECD database was used. The OECD is composed by 36 members, of which 35 were included in this analysis (there was no data available for public investment of Iceland in the OECD database). The countries are: Austria, Australia, Belgium, Brazil, Canada, Chile, China, Colombia, Costa Rica, Czech Republic, Denmark, Estonia, Finland, France, Germany, Greece, Hungary,

And we will divide the tests in **three parts**: 1) **short term** general effects; 2) **long run** general effects; and 3) **distinguish** among different types of countries.

2.4.4.1 Short term general effects

Keynesian policies are supposed to produce results in the short term. That's their aim, since as John M. Keynes put it: *in the long run we are all dead*.

What is the empirical evidence that Keynesian works?

Figures 2-15 and 2-16 provide the answers.

In figure 2-15:

1st: One works with *annual values* (and not the average of the period 2001-2018); and

2nd: The % of public investment (in national income) is correlated with the national income per capita, of 1) that same year, 2) the next year and 3) two years later.

Ireland, Israel, Italy, Japan, Lithuania, Luxembourg, Latvia, Mexico, Netherlands, Norway, New Zealand, Poland, Portugal, Russia, Slovakia, South Africa, Slovenia, Spain, Sweden, Switzerland, South Korea, Turkey, United Kingdom, United States.

Data was also available for 6 other countries. Costa Rica and Colombia are "Candidates for Accession", while Brazil, China and South Africa are "Key Partners" of the OECD. Russia has the status of Associate or Participant in a number of OECD Committees, Working Groups and other bodies.

For the period 2000-2018 values were also retrieved from the OECD database in February 2020 and used in the analysis:

- GNI and GNI per capita—in dollars and current PPPs.

- Total Investment—in dollars and current PPPs, where Investment is defined as Gross Fixed Capital Formation

- General Government Investment as percentage of total investment.

Figure 2-15

Relation between yearly values of % public investment in National Income and National income per capita (period 2000-2018)

Correlation Coefficients / Type / Years	Spearman (ranking)	Pearson (absolute value)
Both variables same year	-0,0531 (0,164)	0,0011 (0,977)
National income per capita next year	-0,0541 (0,165)	-0,0014 (0,971)
National income per capita two years after	-0,0552 (0,170)	-0,0068 (0,867)

Note: 1) Between parentheses significance values.

Source: OECD, Retrieved on February 2020

The results are the inexistence of 1) *high*, 2) *positive* correlations; besides 3) the high probability that whatever the correlations, they are due to chance (values between brackets), all suggesting that **public investment has no significant impact on national income per capita**.

And the conclusions **hold** if instead of working with **absolute** yearly values (figure 2-15) one relates **growth rates** (of the % of public investment in the national income) and national income per capita (figure 2-16).

Indeed, regardless if the growth rates are from the same year, or there is one year leg or two years leg (first, second and third rows, respectively in figure 2-16), there is no evidence for the Keynesian effect.

Relation between annual growth rates of % public investment in national income and the national income per capita (in the period 2000-2018)

Correlation Coefficients / Years	Type	Spearman (ranking)	Pearson (absolute value)
Both variables same year		0,014 (0,728)	0,031 (0,436)
National income per capita next year		0,018 (0,651)	0,017 (0,678)
National income per capita two years after		0,028 (0,497)	0,020 (0,627)

Note: 1) average values for each variable (both in the same year) of each country over the period 2000-2018.

2) Between parentheses significance values.

Source: OECD, Retrieved on February 2020

In short, Keynesianism are short term policies. Aimed at producing results in the near future. Not in the long run. But the results of the tests do not conform to the expectations. **No empirical evidence**.

2.4.4.2 Long run general effects

But what about the *long run?* Could it be that in the long run Keynesian policies are beneficial?

Again we performed two types of tests: for *average* values and rates of *growth.*

Figure 2-17 presents the results for the same sample of countries and period (2000-2018) but now using the average values of the period.

As can be seen from figure 2-17 the values of (both) types of correlation coefficients are neither positive numbers, nor close to +1 as expected and the probability that they are due to chance (between brackets) is very high too: far from zero.

Thus the empirical tests suggest that there is no (positive and strong) **association** between the percentage of public investment in national income and national income per capita and thus we cannot find any evidence for the Keynesian effect.

Figure 2-17

Long term relation between the % of public investment in GNI and National Income per capita (average values of period 2000-2018)

Correlation coefficients	Spearman (Ranking)	Pearson (Absolute Values)
Period 2000-2018	-0,084 (0,60)	0,016 (0,92)

Note: 1) average values for each variable (both in the same year) of each country over the period 2000-2018.
2) Within parentheses significance values.
Source: OECD, Retrieved on February 2020

However if instead of **absolute values**, **rates of growth** are used, **we can indeed find in the long run a beneficial impact of Keynesian programs**. That is what figure 2-18 shows: correlations that are 1) positive, 2) reasonably high, and thus 3) statistically significant at the 10% level (meaning that the probability that they are due to chance is less than 10%).

Long term relation between annual growth rates of % public investment in national income and the national income per capita (in the period 2000-2018)

Correlation Coefficients / Years	Type	Spearman (ranking)	Pearson (absolute value)
Average growth in the period for each country		0,284 (0,071)	0,295 (0,061)

Note: 1) average values for each variable in the period 2000-2018.
2) Between parentheses significance values.
Source: OECD, Retrieved on February 2020

In short, so far we have found **no** support for Keynesian programs in the **short** term. But we have found **some** in the **long** run (over almost two decades).

Here Keynesianism seems to have a positive (although mild) effect[1], most probably because (?) public programs provide countries with better infrastructures thus raising their competitiveness in the long run.

But why is the impact of Keynesian policies so fragile in the short term? Because of the reasons discussed before, namely imports and the burden of borrowing (and therefore having to pay interests on the debt)?

---

[1] Only for growth rates and not averages but even so the correlations are statistically significant only at 10% level: probability of one in ten being due to chance.

2.4.4.3 Distinguishing among several types of countries

To answer those questions figures 2-19 and 2-20 repeat the previous analysis, but now distinguishing among **four** types of countries:

A. With 1) a *large* internal market and 2) an *independent* monetary policy of 3) a currency which is an international *reserve* (USA);

B. A somewhat *smaller* countries but which issue an *international* reserve currency (UK);

C. A *large* country but whose currency is *not* an international reserve (Brazil); and finally

D. *Small* countries such as Portugal, Greece and Ireland *without* an independent monetary policy.

In figure 2-19 the values are for the Spearman (of ranking/order) correlation coefficient and in figure 2-20 for the Pearson (of absolute/cardinal values) correlation coefficient.

In both tables the **first** number next to the country's name is the correlation between **absolute** values and the **second** between **growth rates**.[1]

---

[1] Both the first and second numbers are the simple average of three correlations: same year; one year leg; and two years leg.

Figure 2-19

Spearman correlation between % Public investment in National Income and National Income per capita—growth rates and absolute values (period 2000-2018)

Country	Dimension	Large	Medium or Small
With independent monetary policy or international currency			
		USA	**UK**
Yes	Both variables same year	-0,513 ; -0,569 (0,030 ; 0,017)	0,602 ; 0,327 (0,006 ; 0,185)
	National income per capita next year	-0,523 ; -0,404 (0,026 ; 0,107)	0,602 ; -0,142 (0,008 ; 0,586)
	National income per capita two years after	-0,429 ; 0,071 (0,086 ; 0,795)	0,679 ; 0,309 (0,003 ; 0,244)
		Brazil	**Portugal**
No	Both variables same year	0,453 ; 0,418 (0,068 ; 0,107)	-0,811 ; -0,170 (0,000 ; 0,499)
	National income per capita next year	0,612 ; -0,018 (0,012 ; 0,950)	-0,822 ; - 0,091 (0,000 ; 0,729)
	National income per capita two years after	0,704 ; 0,121 (0,003 ; 0,681)	-0,836 ; -0,244 (0,000 ; 0,405)
			Greece
	Both variables same year		-0,146 ; 0,480 (0,552 ; 0,044)
	National income per capita next year		-0,129 ; 0,108 (0,610 ; 0,680)
	National income per capita two years after		-0,228 ; 0,003 (0,379 ; 0,991)
			Ireland
	Both variables same year		-0,593 ; 0,195 (0,007 ; 0,438)
	National income per capita next year		-0,719 ; -0,176 (0,001 ; 0,498)
	National income per capita two years after		-0,789 ; -0,132 (0,000 ; 0,625)

Note: 1) On the left of (;) is the correlation between absolute values, while on the right is the correlation between annual growth rates.
2) Between parentheses significance values.
Source: OECD, Retrieved on February 2020

Figure 2-20

Pearson correlation between % Public investment in National Income and National Income per capita—growth rates and absolute values (period 2000-2018)

Country / Dimension		Large	Medium or Small
With independent monetary policy or international currency			
		USA	UK
Yes	Both variables same year	-0,620 ; -0,563 (0,006 ; 0,019)	0,619 ; 0,199 (0,005 ; 0,429)
	National income per capita next year	-0,635 ; -0,426 (0,005 ; 0,088)	0,587 ; -0,316 (0,011 ; 0,216)
	National income per capita two years after	-0,550 ; -0,041 (0,022 ; 0,881)	0,604 ; 0,127 (0,010 ; 0,640)
		Brazil	Portugal
No	Both variables same year	0,462 ; 0,551 0,062 ; 0,027)	-0,823 ; 0,014 (0,000 ; 0,955)
	National income per capita next year	0,640 ; 0,076 (0,008 ; 0,787)	-0,844 ; -0,093 (0,000 ; 0,722)
	National income per capita two years after	0,733 ; -0,023 (0,002 ; 0,938)	-0,864 ; -0,404 (0,000 ; 0,121)
			Greece
	Both variables same year		-0,166 ; 0,578 (0,496 ; 0,012)
	National income per capita next year		-0,073 ; 0,203 (0,773 ; 0,434)
	National income per capita two years after		-0,165 ; -0,055 (0,528 ; 0,840)
			Ireland
	Both variables same year		-0,635 ; 0,163 (0,004 ; 0,517)
	National income per capita next year		-0,731 ; -0,162 (0,001 ; 0,535)
	National income per capita two years after		-0,790 ; -0,266 (0,000 ; 0,319)

Note: 1) On the left of (;) is the correlation between absolute values, while on the right is the correlation between annual growth rates.
2) Between parentheses significance values.
Source: OECD, Retrieved on February 2020

As figures 2-19 and 2-20 are complex let's try to **simplify**.

First: **where** do we find 1) *positive*, 2) *high* and 3) statistically *significant* correlations?

In the case of **Brazil** (a country with a large internal market) and the **UK** (medium size country with independent monetary policy and a currency which is international reserve).

Not in small countries such as **Portugal**, **Greece** or **Ireland** where generally the correlations (the associations) are frequently not even positive. These results conform to expectations.

But, **(second):** regarding the above (both in figures 2-19 and 2-20) there is the <u>mild</u> **exception** of **Greece**. Among all twelve correlations for Greece in figures 2-19 and 2-20 there are two exceptions which are statistically significant at 5% level: the correlation 0,48 in figure 2-19 which respects 1) ranking of 2) the same year and 3) growth rate and the rating correlation in figure 2-20 has a value of 0,578.

That may be due (?) to the fact that private investment in Greece is *lowest* among all countries (the % of public investment in total investment highest—see figure 2-21).

Meaning that public investment may have a positive impact on national income only 1) in the same year and 2) regarding growth variables and 3) if the other type of investment, the private one, is *very low*.

Country	Public Investment as % of Total Investment – average values between 2000 and 2018
Ireland	13,21
Brazil	13,46
UK	14,86
Portugal	16,12
USA	17,54
Greece	24,63

Source: OECD, Retrieved on February 2020

Third: the **USA** values are also surprising since, **contrary** to expected, they are negative. The explanation may lie with the high percentage of USA public investment which is nonproductive, namely military expenditures: in the period from 2000 to 2018 the average value of the percentage of **military expenditures** on total public investment was **26%**.

2.4.5 Concluding

In general terms, the previous empirical evidence indicates that, *as trade liberalization increases, the effect of Keynesian public investment policies tend to fade.* Due to imports.

However, there are a few **exceptions**, some instances where Keynesianism still seems to hold:

First: *the long run* (by providing countries with better infrastructures?—see figure 2-18);

Second: when *internal markets are very large* (or the reverse, trade, that is exports + imports, represent a smaller percentage of national income—that is the case of Brazil in figures 2-19 and 2-20);

Third: if the country has 1) an *independent* monetary policy and 2) issues a currency which is an *international reserve* (the UK in figures 2-19 and 2-20); and finally

Fourth: when *private investment* is specially low (Greece in figure 2-21). But even here the **evidence** is very mild.

Finally, the type of public expenditures seems to matter and military nonproductive public expenditures may be an explanation for the inexistence of any evidence of a Keynesian effect in the USA (figures 2-19 and 2-20).

In sum, it is at least dubious that one can rely on Keynesian policies to boost an economy.

So where can we find the source of wealth? In **industrialization**, in increasing the **manufacturing** as many suggest?

Let's turn to the next chapter.

2.5
Industrialization Is Not <u>the</u> Solution to Create Wealth

What counts is not what you do;
it is how you do it.

(-)

2.5.1 Introduction

In the developed world, many economists defend that **industrialization** is <u>the</u> key to create wealth. That national income per capita depends on the weight of **manufacturing** relative to other sectors.

To see how that is pure *nonsense*, let us, first go over the arguments for; then their fallacies; and finally, the empirical evidence.

2.5.2. The arguments

Economies have **four** main sectors. The **primary**: agriculture and extraction (timber, minerals, etc.); the **secondary** (transformation of products: the industry); the **tertiary** (services); and the **most recent** knowledge based sector: internet, e-services, etc.

And nowadays many developed countries have **two** characteristics: the relative weight in national income of the services is high and that of industry **is low** as the manufacturing of products is increasingly transferred to the third and fourth worlds which assume the role of the world's factory.

And the other characteristic is **stagnation**, the so-called Japanese disease: low growth rates.

Since the two factors go together, low growth rates and low importance of industry, many assume that there is a cause-effect relation: that deindustrialization is the reason for low growth.

2.5.3 The fallacies

One of the ways to compute GDP[1] is by adding the value added of firms, being value added the difference between sales and purchases from outside, that is the inputs of raw materials, parts, components, etc.

Productivity is the value added per employee. And *national income per capita* is high when 1) not only *productivity* is high, but also 2) the percentage of *employees* in the active population is also high (there is low unemployment) and 3) the *active* population (those willing to work) are a large percentage of the total population.

And as can be seen in the right side of the formula below, both the number of employees (lines in **green**) and active population (lines in **blue**), cross out as they appear in the numerator and denominator.

The formula is:

$$\frac{\text{National income (sum of valued added)}}{\text{Total population}} = \frac{\text{National income (sum of values added)}}{\text{Number of employees}} \times \frac{\text{Number of employees}}{\text{Active population}} \times \frac{\text{Active population}}{\text{Total population}}$$

| National income per capita | Productivity | Rate of employment (1 − rate of unemployment) | Rate of activity |

---

[1] The other is by adding the remuneration of all resources: labor (wages), land (rents) and capital (interests and profits). As referred in chapter 2.1.

So, both productivity and national income per capita, they come down to **value added**. That is what is **critical**.

Thus the question: is there anything **intrinsic** to (in the "DNA" of) industry which induces its value added to be (necessarily) high? Or to facilitate considerably the creation of high value added per employee?

And the answer is: **of course not**. If one sells low price textiles, value added is low; if one sells fashion (Gucci, Versace, etc.), value added is high. And both belong to the **industrial sector**.

If a country's hospitality business is composed mostly of motels and two and three stars hotels, then value added is low; but if hotels are primarily five stars, luxury, charm hotels, then value added is high. And all belong to the **service sector**.

That means that there are high and low value added goods both in products and services. Whatever. And that regardless of the sector, value added is a consequence of applying scarce resources to goods which are sold because of their quality (intrinsic or image) or/and delivery and not based on their cost, price.

It could be however (for some reason) far easier to create high value goods in manufacturing rather than in services.

If so, the **richest countries would have a greater relative weight of industry in the national income, than the poorer ones**.

That is, between both variables there would be a correlation 1) *positive*, 2) *high* (close to +1), and 3) statistically *significant* (the number between brackets in the following figures, representing the probability that the correlation value is due to chance should be low).

Is that so?

2.5.4 The empirical evidence

Figure 2-22 presents the **correlation coefficients Spearman** (rank, order) and **Pearson** (cardinal) for several samples of countries starting with smaller samples where, by being countries more homogeneous, it is harder to expect strong and significant correlations. And then moving into more diverse samples:

    1st—The 20 richest countries;
    2nd—The most advanced economies[1];
    3rd—The 20 poorer countries;
    4th—The emerging markets and developing economies;
    5th—Both the 20 richer and poorer;
    6th—The 20 wealthier and the far east;

And then larger samples of:
    7th—Total of 191 countries[2], excluding and
    8th—Including oil producer countries.

---

[1] The IMF distinguishes between advanced economies, on one hand and emerging markets and developing economies, on the other, based on (1) per capita income level, (2) export diversification—so oil exporters that have high GDP per capita would not make the advanced classification because around 70% of its exports are oil, and (3) degree of integration into the global financial system. In 2019, the group "advanced economies", as defined by the World Economic Outlook is composed by 39 countries, namely Australia, Austria, Belgium, Canada, Cyprus, Czech Republic, Denmark, Estonia, Finland, France, Germany, Greece, Hong Kong SAR, Iceland, Ireland, Israel, Italy, Japan, Korea, Latvia, Lithuania, Luxembourg, Macao SAR, Malta, Netherlands, New Zealand, Norway, Portugal, Puerto Rico, San Marino, Singapore, Slovak Republic, Slovenia, Spain, Sweden, Switzerland, Taiwan Province of China, United Kingdom, and United States.

[2] All 191 countries for which the World Bank and World Economic Outlook databases had information available.

And as per figure 2-22, the correlation coefficients are **only** 1) positive, 2) high and 3) statistically significant in lines **four** (sample of emerging markets and developing economies) and partially in **eight**: the total sample of countries, where only the Spearman (rank/order) but not the Pearson (cardinal) correlation is significant.

In **all other cases** they are **small** and with a high probability of being due to **chance**; sometimes the correlations are even negative and statistically significant, indicating that—contrary to the argument—the higher the industry percentage in national income, the lower its per capita. That is the case with the Pearson correlation on the first line (sample of 20 richest countries): the less manufacturing, the higher the income.

Figure 2-22

Correlation coefficients between % of industry in national income and national income per capita

Samples		Type of correlation [4]	
		Spearman	**Pearson**
1	The 20 richest countries[1]	-0,218 (0,356)	-0,412 (0,071)
2	The most advanced economies [2]	-0,053 (0,748)	-0,230 (0,159)
3	The 20 poorer countries	-0,083 (0,729)	-0,140 (0,556)
4	The emerging markets and developing economies	0,372 (0,000)	0,472 (0,000)
5	The 20 richer[1] + 20 poorer	0,166 (0,305)	0,084 (0,607)
6	The 20 richer[1] and the far east	-0,516 (0,003)	-0,613 (0,000)
7	Total of 191[3] countries excluding the 20 oil producer countries with the largest % of GDP that comes from oil[2]	0,127 (0,0988)	0,016 (0,836)
8	Total of 191 countries including oil producer countries [3]	0,203 (0,005)	0,176 (0,015)

Notes:

(1) 20 countries with the highest GDP per capita, not considering the 20 countries with the highest percentage of GDP that comes from oil.

(2) The IMF distinguishes between advanced economies, on one hand and emerging markets and developing economies, on the other, based on (1) per capita income level, (2) export diversification – so oil exporters that have high GDP per capita would not make the advanced classification because around 70% of its exports are oil, and (3) degree of integration into the global financial system. In 2019, the group "advanced economies", as defined by the World Economic Outlook is composed by 39 countries, namely Australia, Austria, Belgium, Canada, Cyprus, Czech Republic, Denmark, Estonia, Finland, France, Germany, Greece, Hong Kong SAR, Iceland, Ireland, Israel, Italy, Japan, Korea, Latvia, Lithuania, Luxembourg, Macao SAR, Malta, Netherlands, New Zealand, Norway, Portugal, Puerto Rico, San Marino, Singapore, Slovak

Republic, Slovenia, Spain, Sweden, Switzerland, Taiwan Province of China, United Kingdom, and United States.

(3) All 191 countries for which the World Bank and World Economic Outlook databases had information available.

(4) Between brackets: the level of statistical significance.

Source: World Bank, July 2019; World Economic Outlook, April 2019.

So in general, not only the data does **not support** that there is a positive relation between the importance of the industry and a country's wealth, but also there is an indication that among the twenty richest countries it is the **opposite** which happens.

But **why** the two **exceptions** (in lines four and eight)?

Starting with line **four** (emerging markets and developing economies), these are countries whose economy is based in 1) agriculture, 2) with family farms, 3) using traditional methods, 4) frequently exploiting small lots.

When industry is introduced, even if *factories* produce low cost items, that represents nevertheless an **improvement** in terms of value added by employee (productivity) and inhabitant (per capita). Even because some of those factories are managed directly or at least to some degree controlled by first world *multinationals*, which bring to those manufacturing units its management expertise.

Then there is the **second** exception: line **eight**, the total sample of countries, and here the correlation is positive and significant (with only a 5% probability of being due to chance) in the Spearman/rank/order coefficient, but not in the Pearson/cardinal (lower value and 15% of probability of being due to chance).

The reason is that the sample includes oil producing countries. Oil is a high value commodity. And the petroleum industry involves not only extraction (primary sector), but also refining and distributing its by-products, gasoline, diesel, etc. (secondary sector).

Indeed, when the exceptional impact of oil is taken into account by removing the oil rich countries from the sample (the 7th line in figure 2-22), the values of both the (Spearman and Pearson) correlations fall and become nonsignificant.

2.5.5 Conclusion

As per figure 2-22, **except** for the case of **very poor** economies shifting from traditional, family based agricultural units to factories (frequently managed by first world companies) and **the oil effect**, **there is no relation, whatsoever, between wealth and industry**. And on the contrary: among the twenty richest countries, the importance of manufacturing is associated with lower income per capita.

The diagram of figure 2-23 emphasizes the point. If there was a relation, as the countries' wealth per capita increases from the left to the right (in **green**), the industry weight in economy (**red** line) would move in parallel, or at least in the same way. But that is not what happens. The green and red lines do not have the same trend.[1]

---

[1] Figure 2-23 uses the gross domestic product and not national income for reasons of data availability.

Figure 2-23

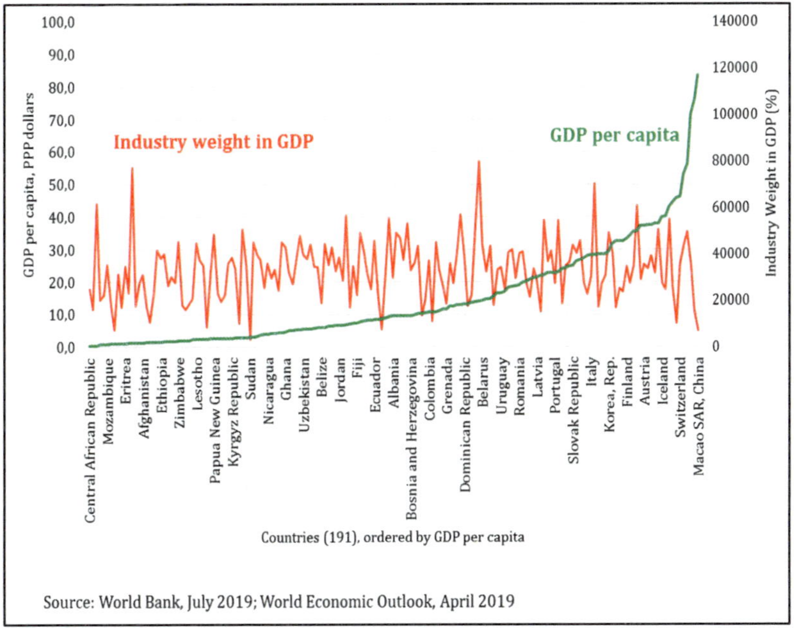

And thus so much for (re)industrialization as the source of wealth.

And industrialization joins the **non-solutions** analyzed in the previous chapters.

Where does all that leaves us?

To the **conclusion**, next.

2.6
Conclusion

Denial does not change reality
but can make it deadly.

Andy Grove (former Intel CEO and chairman)

Economics has long enjoyed a **special status** among social sciences. Since we feel its effects every single day. And because we are supplied with *"solutions"* based on reasonable complex mathematical models under a great aura of formality.

Notwithstanding, economic progress requires both **efficiency** (doing things right) and **effectiveness** (doing the right things).

And to achieve the latter one must first know what the non-solutions are, the irrelevant, in order to be able to focus on what truly, really, matters.

Indeed frequently, **the problem** is **not** what we don't know, but what we think that it is and it ain't so.

That is, the **non-solutions** we rely upon and that fail to deliver. The first part of this book analyzed **five** of them[1].

First, the gross domestic product is an obsolete indicator of how an economy is evolving. *Luxembourg, Ireland, Portugal*, among others, are examples of why GDP is today a dangerous statistic: it gives no forewarning and consequently fails to induce the action which would prevent problems from becoming emergencies.

---

[1] Every field has its myths. For instance business administration also has its large collection of fables. Peter Drucker, founder of modern management, used to say that many received the title of gurus, because charlatans is harder to spell.

National income (as per chapter *2.1*) is a far better statistic than **gross domestic product.** However, few institutions use it.

Also, one cannot either rely on **economic unions** with their advantages of free trade, economies of scale, etc. to bring economic **convergence**. Indeed the opposite happens: countries within (e.g.) the European Union and the federal states of the USA tend to **diverge**: the **gap** between the richer and the poorer increases (chapter *2.2*).

And that is a problem that **financial flows** from the richer to the poorer do not solve either (chapter *2.3*).

In fact, after receiving almost fifty billion euros and 4% of their income during a quarter century, the poorest European countries failed, not only to converge with the richest, but even generally **worsened** in their world rankings of *transparency, economic freedom* and *economic competitiveness*.

If economic blocks and central financing fail to deliver, the same happens with **Keynesian public programs** in the **short term**. Only in the long run (almost two decades) and in a few other exceptional instances, is there some, mild, evidence of their results (chapter *2.4*).

Finally, there is no empirical evidence of the importance of **industry** and **manufacturing** in creating wealth. And thus, so much for the argument of **reindustrializing** the most developed economies (chapter *2.5*).

Nevertheless to increase productivity remains extremely *important*, among others, for **three** reasons.

First, we live in a world where there is still much **poverty**: 1/4 of the world population lives with less than 3,2 dollars per day and 1/10 with less than 1,9 dollars[1].

Then, in developed countries the ratio of **active** population over retirees has been constantly decreasing at the (annual) rate of -2,2% and -1,8% in the USA and Europe, respectively (figure 2-24). What naturally requires that those working be ever more productive.

And finally the **costs of healthcare** rise steadily in the last years of life (figure 2-25). Thus, greater life expectancy requires more resources, which must come from higher productivity.

Figure 2-24

Sources: Eurostat; FRED, Federal Reserve Bank of St. Louis; Statistical Annex of European Economy, European Commission. Searched in March 2020

Note: The ratio is computed by dividing working age population (15 to 64 years) by older dependents (65 years and over), who is assumed to be the average age of retirees among countries. Thus, it is the inverse of the "Age dependency ratio, Old".

---

[1] Source: World Bank.

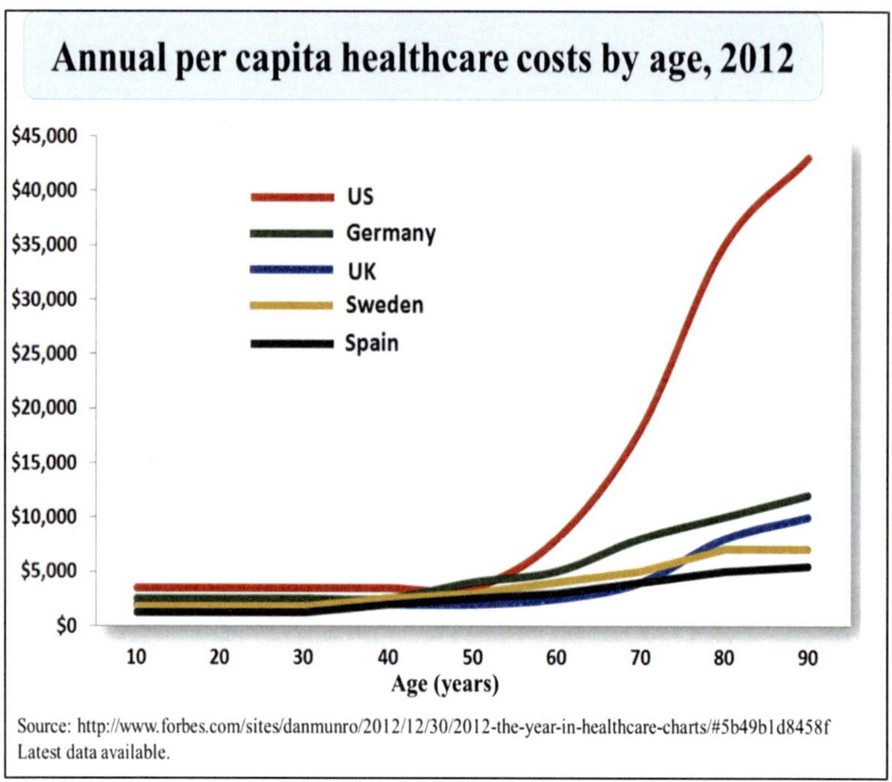

Economics is thus **important** for reasons well **beyond** the *standard of living*: for reasons which include *life expectancy, quality of life,* the *safety* net of social security and our *generosity* to the needy, as there are some virtues that only the rich can have.

We thus need economic progress. To create wealth. Being the first step to recognize the **non-solutions**, as only by keeping away from them, are we able to select the right path.

That is **effectiveness** and not only **efficiency**: **to do the right things, besides doing them right.**

Otherwise one aims at competence in the irrelevant which constitutes a double loss: of effort (resources) and results (wealth).

Half a century ago, **Peter Drucker** said that **there is nothing as stupid as doing well the irrelevant**. Translated to economics, that means not to be entangled in **economic myths**.

Once they are put aside and dispelled, one can then turn to the fundamental question of what really matters for economic growth: what are the sources of wealth?

For the answer, let's turn to the **second part of the book**.

III
Economic Realities: The Real Sources of Economic Growth

Facts are obstinate; they do not cease to exist only because they are ignored.

Aldous Huxley

3.1
Our Ignorance on the Sources of Economic Growth

I would like to know if there is some action the government of India could take that would lead the Indian economy to grow; what exactly?

Robert Lucas (Nobel Prize winner)

3.1.1 Introduction

A few years ago I gave a conference in a developing country on how Peter Drucker's ideas, founder of modern management, are still relevant in today's world.

The keynote speaker was Paul Krugman, the Nobel Prize winner and reputed New York Times columnist.

At a certain moment to the utter amazement of the audience, Krugman candidly stated that economists do not know the sources of economic growth.

A statement, as will be seen next, shared by many other well-known economists. For understandable reasons. But nevertheless tragic since, as Robert Lucas in the previously quoted Marshall[1] lecture put it: "the consequences for human welfare are simply staggering; once one starts to think about them, it is hard to think about anything else."

So the question is why?

Let's divide the answer in 1) *facts*; 2) *reasons*; and 3) *solution*.

---

[1] Robert E. Lucas Jr., "On the Mechanics of Economic Development", *Journal of Monetary Economics* 22, no. I (1988): pp. 3-42

3.1.2 The facts

Four facts stand out.

First, absolute poverty has been *decreasing*. Indeed, the fraction of those living under 1,9 dollars a day has been halved since 1990[1].

In spite of that, however, poverty is still *prevalent* as almost 1/4 of the world's population lives with less than 3,2 dollars a day and 1/10 with less than 1,9 dollars. [2]

Third, income *disparities* remain high. The richest top ten countries[3] (excluding those whose main export is oil) have a per capita income fifty nine (!) times that of the bottom ten (see figure 3-1).

---

[1] "Poverty", World Bank, 2019, accessed April 14, 2019, https://www.worldbank.org/en/topic/poverty/overview#1.

[2] World Bank.

[3] Excluding countries whose main export is oil, the top ten are: Macao SAR, Singapore, Norway, Switzerland, Hong Kong SAR, Luxembourg, United States, San Marino, Netherlands and Iceland. And the bottom ten: Madagascar, Sierra Leone, South Sudan, Liberia, Mozambique, Niger, Malawi, Congo Democratic Republic, Burundi and Central African Republic (see figure 3-1).

Figure 3-1

Comparing the income per capita of the world's top and bottom ten countries

	Countries	GDP per capita PPP (dollars)	Ratio of top ten over bottom ten:
T O P T E N (NO OIL)	Macao SAR	116808	
	Singapore	100345	
	Norway	74356	
	Switzerland	64649	
	Hong Kong SAR	64216	
	Luxembourg	64023	
	United States	62606	
	San Marino	60313	
	Netherlands	56383	
	Iceland	55023	
	AVERAGE	**71872**	**59**
B O T T O M T E N	Madagascar	1630	
	Sierra Leone	1620	
	South Sudan	1502	
	Liberia	1418	
	Mozambique	1291	
	Niger	1217	
	Malawi	1199	
	Dem. Rep. of the Congo	767	
	Burundi	733	
	Central African Republic	712	
	AVERAGE	**1209**	

Source: IMF; 2019

Notes: (1) For a total of 191 countries; (2) The values of Luxembourg and Ireland GDP per capita were decreased with the corrections analyzed in chapter 2.1.

Finally, the general trend is toward *divergence*, not convergence. Both in terms of countries and people.

In terms of countries, the correlation between income per capita in 1960 and the subsequent rate of growth is near zero. [1]

---

[1] J. Bradford De Long, "Productivity Growth, Convergence, and Welfare: Comment", *American Economic Review* 78, no. 5 (1988): 1138-54 and at www.bradford-delong.com/2015/08/in-which-i-once-again-bet-on-a-substancial-growth-slowdown-in-china.html.

And in terms of people although the income of the bottom 50% in the world has been growing faster than the others 49%, the top one percent, the very rich, did even better, since they obtained 27% of the world's income (against 13% for the bottom 50%).[1]

In sum, although absolute poverty has been decreasing, divergence not only remains high, but is even increasing.

And once we ask why, the answer is that there are **immediate**, direct causes, and **original**, primary, ones.

3.1.3 The immediate causes

As per figure 3-2 the gross domestic product per capita is the consequence of the multiplication of **four** factors:

1st—*Productivity per hour* (GDP divided by hour);

2nd—*Average number of hours* worked by employees (total number of hours divided by employed population);

Being that these two factors together result in the productivity per employed person since the total number of hours worked cross out in the numerator and in the denominator;

3rd—*The activity rate* (ratio of actives divided by the total population); and finally

4th—*The rate of employment* (that is 100% minus the rate of unemployment): the quotient between the employed population and the active one).

---

[1] Facundo Alvaredo, Lucas Chancel, Thomas Piketty, Emmanuel Saez, and Gabriel Zucman, "World Inequality Report 2018: Executive Summary", World Inequality Lab, 2018.

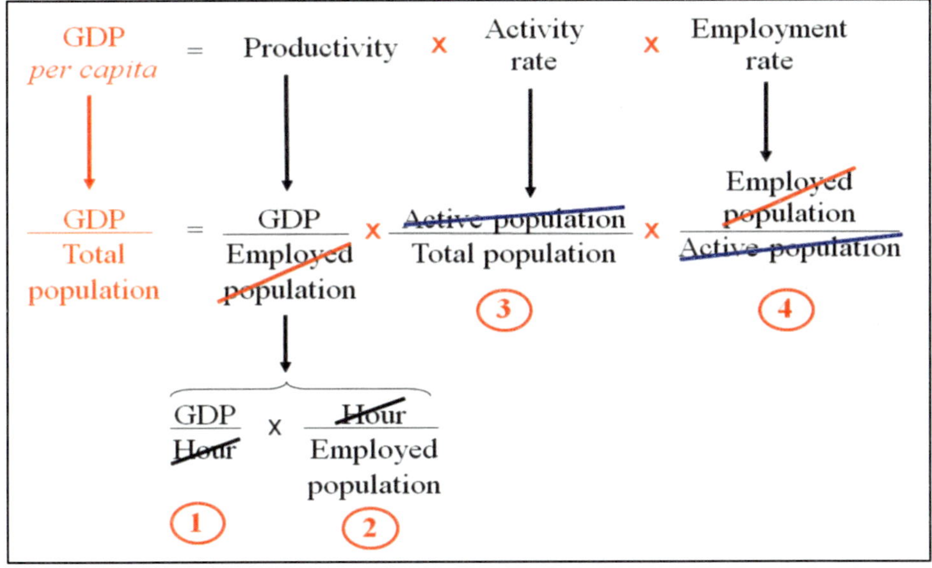

As can be seen from left to the right in figure 3-2, hours cross out (diagonal line in black) and so do employed population (line in red) and active population (line in blue), leaving solely the value of GDP per capita (GDP divided by total population).

Thus a country's population standard of living depends on its **age** (percentage of actives), **employment** rate and **productivity**[1].

That is, what determines a country's competitiveness, is exemplified in figure 3-3 for Portugal, whose income per capita is only 73,6% of EU-15 average (far right column) for EU-15 = 100%.

---

[1] Being the difference per employee and per hour explained by the number of hours worked.

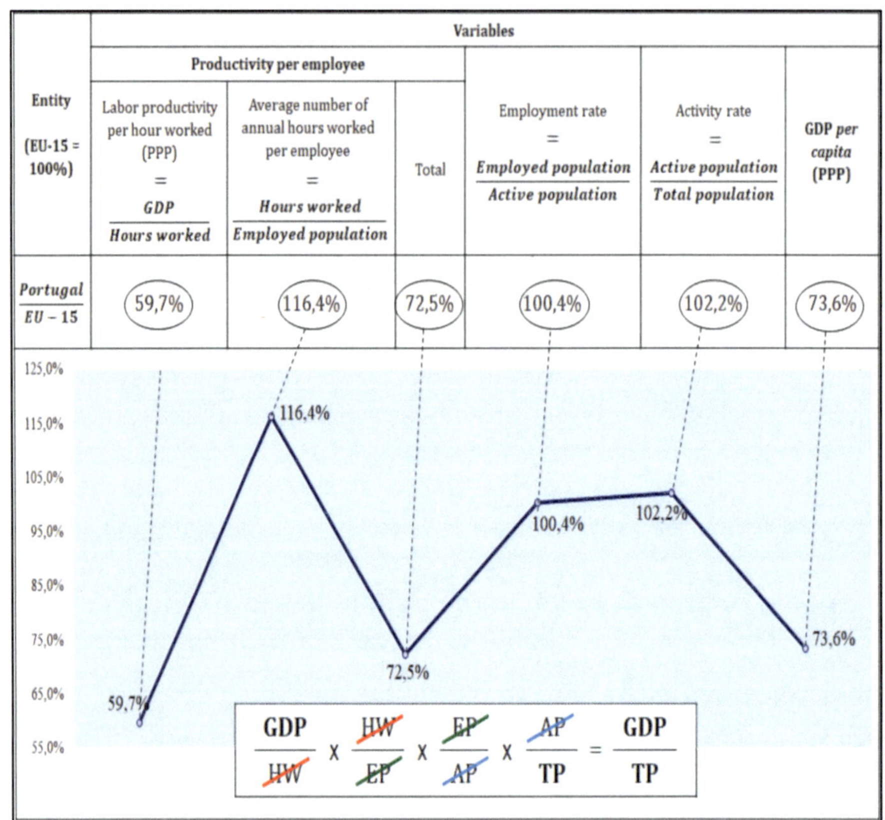

Source: AMECO

Why?

Not due to a far lower percentage of actives, since compared to the EU, Portugal has more 2,2% actives in its population (thus the value 102,2% in the second right column).

Neither because of inferior rate of employment as Portuguese and EU's are quite similar (Portugal is even 0,4% above—third column from right).

And so the explanation must be found in the difference of productivity per employee which in Portugal is solely 72,5% of EU average (third column from the left).

But again why? The explanation lies in the first two columns: although Portuguese work 16,4% more hours than Europeans (second column from left), their product per hour is only 59,7% that of an average European (left column).

In short, because Portuguese produce per hour little more than half the average European does and consequently in spite of working more hours (+16%) and having more actives (more 2%) and even slightly higher employment (+0,4%), Portuguese income per capita is less than 3/4 (73,6%) of Europe's average.

If the example of Portugal demonstrates the direct, immediate, causes of income per capita, it does however leave unanswered the key question of why is (e.g.) Portuguese productivity so low?

And what can countries do to increase their productivity and rate of employment, that is their overall competitiveness, the engine of economic growth?

What causes the level of productivity and employment? What are the **original** causes? The causes of the… causes?

3.1.4 The original causes

Here our analysis should be divided between what we know and what we don't know.

3.1.4.1 What we know

There is a general consensus on three facts: in some exceptional circumstances *one* factor is enough (it is a *sufficient* condition); then *two* other factors have been *losing* importance (to the point that today they can be considered false causes); and finally a third type of policies is to be avoided under all circumstances.

3.1.4.1.1 Exceptional circumstances creating a single sufficient condition

First of all in a few exceptional instances a *single factor* is *enough* for high income per capita.

That happens regarding 1) very *small* countries (in terms of population) which are richly endowed with 2) *oil*.

That explains why (in figure 3-4) Qatar is the richest country in the world, Brunei is the 4th, UAE the 6th and Kuwait the 7th.

Figure 3-4

Top 20 countries in terms of income per capita

Ranking	Country	GDP per capita PPP, 2018 (dollars)
1	Qatar	130475
2	Macao SAR	116808
3	Singapore	100345
4	Brunei Darussalam	79530
5	Norway	74356
6	United Arab Emirates	69382
7	Kuwait	67000
8	Switzerland	64649
9	Hong Kong SAR	64216
10	Luxembourg	64023
11	United States	62606
12	San Marino	60313
13	Netherlands	56383
14	Saudi Arabia	55944
15	Iceland	55917
16	Taiwan	53023
17	Sweden	52984
18	Germany	52559
19	Australia	52373
20	Austria	52137

Source: IMF, April 2019; Total = 191 countries

Note: Data derived by dividing GDP in PPP dollars by total population; The values of Luxembourg and Ireland GDP per capita were decreased with the corrections analyzed in chapter 2.1.

However when one of the two conditions, small population <u>and</u> high oil reserves are not present, very high income per capita does not follow automatically.

That is the case of Saudi Arabia which having a more sizable population (35 million) ranks 14th and most specially of Venezuela. Although it possesses the largest oil reserves in the world, it is the 3rd poorer South American country (after Bolivia and Guyana), being the richer Chile, Uruguay and Argentina. All three far less blessed in terms of natural resources and location.

Brazil ranks as world number one in sugar, coffee and many other agricultural products, number two in iron ore, 4th in wood, 7th in tin, 9th in oil and 13th in gold. But its population of 230 million lower its rank to 85th in terms of income per capita. Other examples are Libya (108th in the world), Angola (131st) and Nigeria (136th).[1]

Anyway five of the top ten richest countries in figure 3-4, Macao, Singapore, Switzerland, Hong Kong and Luxembourg, have no extensive highly valuable mineral resources, much less oil.

And the same happens with nine of the next ten wealthier countries (the sole exception is Saudi Arabia).

So what explains their wealth?

3.1.4.2 The false causes

That question leads to the second fact that we know, namely what the source of wealth is **not**: the non-answers, the two false causes of **location** and **climate**.

---

[1] Norway (5th) is also a major oil exporter but not mono-exporter, as it exports are roughly equally divided between mineral fuels related materials, such as petroleum and natural gas and the other 50% composed by fish products, machinery, transport equipment and chemicals.

Formerly a country's location could be a strong advantage or disadvantage, influencing the degree to which a society was open or isolated and thus more or less in contact with other cultures for cross fertilization of ideas and trade benefits.

Today however, with the death of distance, **location** has become far less relevant.

McLuhan baptized the term global village to portrait an ever nearer and "smaller" world consequence of improvements in transportation (speed, flexibility and cost) and communications (internet, mobile, social media, etc.).

That means that location can still be a handicap only in very extreme circumstances such as small islands in the Pacific (Nauru), the Atlantic island of Tristao da Cunha, or Greenland, an autonomous territory belonging to Denmark, which, due to extreme conditions of weather, darkness and solitude, among other factors, has one of the worlds higher alcoholism and suicide rates.

However, extreme cases aside, location is an increasingly minor fact. Finland at the geographic extreme of Europe, has a national income per capita 3% above EU-15[1] average and is the 27th wealthiest world country.

When Akio Morita, founder of Sony, mentioned (but not complained) about Japan's bad location he did have a point: Japan is a discontinued territory of several islands, in the high north of the Asian continent and neighboring Siberia. Nevertheless Japan ranks 31st in income in the world.

Iceland in the northern and New Zealand in the southern hemispheres are two other examples of the death of distance. Both

---

[1] Including former EU member Great Britain.

geographically isolated, they nevertheless rank as the 15th and 34th richest countries in the world, respectively.

And then there is by far the worst located country of all southern America, isolated from all the others by the Andes: Chile. However, not only it has an income per capita 70% above South America's average, but also it is the wealthiest country in all (northern, central and south) American continent, with the exception of the USA, Canada and a few Caribbean tourist and fiscal paradises[1].

So due to technology, location has been losing its previous prominence. And the same happens with **climate**.

Sure that it can still play a role, be it due to 1) *instability* (frequency of tornados and storms), 2) *extreme cold* (which increases the difficulty of all types of communications), or still 3) the *reverse*, very high temperatures, leading some to speak of an equatorial range of underdevelopment.

However modern climatization techniques allowing for the insulation from the environment, explains why Singapore whose year average temperature during the day is 32 degrees Celsius and Taiwan which has a medium of 22 degrees Celsius, and a brutally hot and high humid summer, rank worldwide in income per capita as 3rd and 16th respectively.

So location and climate do not play such an important role as before. But there is a third factor whose relevance is timeless. Not as a positive strength. But as something to shun away from. At all costs.

---

[1] Bahamas, Aruba, Puerto Rico, Trinidad & Tobago, Saint Kitts & Nevis and Antigua & Barbuda.

3.1.4.3 What to avoid

Milton Friedman's similar advice to two very different cultures, stress what to dodge.

In his letters to both general secretary Zhao Ziyang (of China) and general Pinochet Ugarte (of Chile), Friedman recommended two types of policies which came to be validated, not by doctrine, but by their results. And policies are like remedies: what counts is not their taste but their results.

First, to end **inflation** by controlling the rate of growth of the quantity of money.

And second to increase **market freedom**, that is the role that 1) private and 2) free markets play in the economy.

The latter requires that externally exchange rates controls be abandoned to allow rates to be determined freely by the market; and internally, besides again deregulating individual prices and wages, to privatize many activities performed by the centralized government and state enterprises.

In short, lack of freedom[1] is to be avoided, since as Friedman reminded in his memorandum to the general secretary Zhao Ziyang,

---

[1] Market freedom both enables and requires specialization. As B. Appelbaum in his book The Economists Hour (Little Brown & Co) reports "There are few theories that command such broad agreement among economists as the assertion that free trade benefits all participating nations… a YouTube video featuring Andy George, a man who decided to make his own sandwich. documented the process of growing his own lettuce and wheat, evaporating ocean water for salt, milking a cow, killing a chicken. The sandwich took six months to make and cost $1500. McDonald's, meanwhile, sells chicken sandwiches for less than $5. The point is that specialization saves time and money. One person writes for money and buys food, another makes food and buys books; the result is more food and books. The same logic holds for a community, for a nation, and for the global economy".

many decades ago, before the Russian revolution and the end of the Chinese civil war, what did work and did not work could be subject to some degree of controversy.

The absence of large empirical evidence opened the room for theoretical arguments. Today not so anymore. Centralized planning, with its theoretical qualities of organization, failed to produce results comparable to the chaotic and unplanned market economies, dominated by uncoordinated individual actions whose single purpose is to promote their self-interest.

Friedman argued that much in the seventies and eighties. But henceforth, empirical evidence has but strengthened the argument.

South Korea is the 32nd richest country in the world. North Korea? The 180th.

Cuba, in spite of its booming tourism, ranks 118th, while Bahamas is 45th, Trinidad and Tobago 46th, Antigua and Barbuda 56th, Panama 62nd, Barbados 75th, Dominican Republic 77th, Costa Rica 82nd, Grenada 84th, and so on.

The partial opening and privatization of China improved its performance to such a degree that it is frequently considered a success.

But compared to what?

After all it ranks 78th in the world in income per capita against Macao which is number two, Singapore (also strongly ethnic Chinese) number three, Hong Kong 9th and Taiwan 16th.

One should note, however, that when putting aside statism, privatization is not enough. Markets must also be free to allow for consumer sovereignty in choosing the best supplier in terms of price, quantity and delivery. That is, there must be strong competition within private markets. Few monopolies, oligopolies and dominant firms.

And, as D. Landes noted[1], liberty increases diversity, which is a source of wealth. Then, in top of that, survival in competitive markets require social virtues, as Fukuyama (author of the famous books The End of History and the Last Man) defends in his book *Trust*[2]. Social ethics are fundamental for prosperity as they encourage transactions and enable the benefits of specialization[3].

Friedman in his autobiography (Two Lucky People) makes a similar argument: freedom is the greatest protection against discrimination, which is at the opposite pole of a culture of merit.

In short, it is known that statism does not work, neither do private markets unless they are free to allow competition equally from external and internal sources. As many Latin American and African countries exemplify.

3.1.4.4 Summing up

There are a *few exceptional circumstances* when the match between low population and plentiful of **oil**, is sufficient for wealth. That is

---

[1] David S. Landes, "The Wealth and Poverty of Nations: Why Some Are So Rich and Some So Poor", Little, Brown and Company (1995).
In this book the Harvard professor David Landes defends diversity, openness, as they enable exposure to new ideas and trade. And stresses the importance of non-segregation of minorities and women's participation in the workforce, having the latter two effects: a quantitative one increasing the active population and thus national income per capita and a qualitative effect since women bring different characteristics to the workforce, complementing men's.
[2] Francis Fukuyama, "Trust: The Social Virtues and the Creation of Prosperity", The Free Press (1995).
[3] Besides other advantages now in the social field. In his autobiography (Two Lucky People) Friedman argues that freedom and private markets are the best defense against discrimination.

the case of four among the ten richest countries in the world: Qatar, Brunei, UAE and Kuwait in figure 3-4.

And it is also known that technology progress has decreased the importance of **location** and **climate**.

And statism in lieu of **privatization** rather than freedom should be avoided.

The above facts do leave however unanswered the fundamental question of what explains the ratio of 59 in figure 3-1, between the ten richest and poorest world countries? And why countries absolutely destitute of natural resources, such as Singapore, Switzerland and Luxembourg, rank numbers three, eight and ten in the world?

The answer is that so far empirical evidence has remained elusive.

3.1.4.5 The elusive empirical evidence

The Nobel winner *Robert Lucas*[1], openly confessed his embarrassment when visiting a third world country and in the usual audience with the Prime Minister he is asked the (also usual) question: what should I do to increase the pace of my country's economic growth?

At that time (1987) *Robert Solow* had won the Nobel Prize for his work on the theory of economic growth and produced a model which explained 37% of the income variance: 10% due to the

---

[1] Robert E. Lucas Jr., "On the Mechanics of Economic Development", *Journal of Monetary Economics* 22, no. I (1988): pp. 3-42

number of man-hours fulltime and 27% to capital stock. And the remaining 63%, Solow defined as the *measure of our ignorance.*[1]

Three decades later, in 2018, *Paul Romer* received a Nobel for complementing Solow's exogenous sources of growth (man-hours plus capital), with the endogenous cause of the dissemination of knowledge among the population, in terms of R&D, patents and entrepreneurship.[2]

Paul Romer's theory has the advantage of explaining why—in spite of the potential diminishing returns of physical capital—such great wealth differences persist among countries across the world.[3]

It has, however, the serious drawback, that one has so far been unable to validate the theory with strong empirical evidence: only 58% of the difference in GDP per capita growth among countries was explained.[4]

---

[1] Robert M. Solow, "Growth Theory: an exposition", Oxford Clarendon Press (1970)

Robert M. Solow, "A Contribution to the Theory of Economic Growth", *The Quarterly Journal of Economics*, vol 70, no. 1 (1956): pp. 65-94

Robert M. Solow, "Applying Growth Theory across Countries", *The World Bank Economic Review*, vol. 15, no. 2 (2001): pp. 283-288

Robert M. Solow, "Technical Change and the Aggregate Production Function", *The Review of Economics and Statistics,* vol. 39, no. 3, The MIT Press (1957): pp. 312-20

Robert M. Solow, "Capital Theory and the Rate of Return", North-Holland Publishing Company (1963)

[2] Paul M. Romer, "Dynamic competitive equilibria with externalities, increasing returns and unbounded growth" (Ph.D.), *The University of Chicago* (1983)

Paul M. Romer, "Increasing returns and long-run growth", *Journal of Political Economy*, vol. 94, no. 5 (1986): pp. 1002-1037

[3] Paul M. Romer, "Economic Growth", *The Concise Encyclopedia of Economics*, Indianapolis, Ind., Liberty Fund (2008)

[4] Paul M. Romer, "Human capital and growth: Theory and evidence", *Carnegie-Rochester Conference Series on Public Policy*, Volume 32 (1990): pp. 251-286.

Although naturally many other empirical studies were done, they all suffer, however, from one or more of the following limitations: 1) not using GDP per capita of the total population as dependent variable; 2) low results; 3) narrow samples; or 4) an unclear theory justifying the choice of the causal variables. [1]

---

[1] Empirical research on the sources of economic growth can be divided into **four** categories.

First, Solow's ground breaking and Nobel winning work in 1963, which using as sample USA data of the years 1929-1957 and with capital and man-hours as independent variables, explained 37% of the GNP absolute (not per capita) variance.

Second, there is Paul Romer, another Nobel winner, who under his endogenous theory explains a higher variance of GDP per capita: 58%. It includes as an independent variable 1960 GNP per capita for the sample countries, assuming decreasing marginal productivity of capital, what requires to focus on the quantity, not quality of capital.

A **third** category of empirical studies includes G. Mankiw et al, K.B. Grier et al, S. Zhu et al, R. Barro and R. Kavoussi.

The former achieved a R^2 of 78% but with as dependent variable GDP per capita of the active, not of the total population, and human capital was operationalized with the extent of secondary education, leaving outside higher education and professional training (as will be done in this book).

Then, Grier's analysis produced an 82% R^2 but with absolute GDP, not per capita, and using as an independent variable the population growth.

Still, Zhu's work explains 70% in the short term and 40% in the long run, variance, but again of absolute, not per capita, GDP.

Next, Barro's R^2 is 76%, but the theory behind the independent variables choice is not clear as it includes life expectancy, perhaps better suited to be a dependent variable, or if used as an independent variable it can both be argued to have a positive or negative contribution (higher level of pensioners).

And Kavoussi obtained a R^2 between 58% and 78% depending on the sample being larger (73 countries) or smaller (36), but regarding developing countries only, excluding OECD countries. This book will consider, both developed and developing countries.

There is finally the **fourth** category of studies which focus on the impact of a single cause on GDP per capita. That is the case of Raghutla which concluded that 1% increase in trade implies a 18,6% augment on the GDP growth rate and Benhabib

Examples of the latter are the competitiveness indexes developed by the NGOs World Economic Forum[1] and Institute of Management Development[2]. Although in both cases their correlation with GDP per capita is 0,9, the indexes do however have two disadvantages.

First, a long list of **more than one hundred** variables as possible causes. For instance the latest IMD index uses 334 variables grouped in 20 pillars (subfactors).

And **second**, the possibility of **spurious relations** between them and the GDP per capita: in the absence of a strong theory which justifies the choice of every single variable, there is the risk that they are both a consequence of third variables, the real causes.

Ice creams consumption and the number of drownings are associated. Their numbers move together, up and down. But obviously neither causes the other as they are the simple consequence of a third variable: temperature.

In Holland the number of stork nests has its peak in the spring when the birth rate is maximum too. Although that explains the origin of the idea that storks bring babies, causality is nevertheless also absent. The first fact is a consequence of nature. And the second that nine months have passed since the last summer.

---

et al. that focusing on human capital obtained disappointing results as the parameters came negative in some instances and not significant in others.

In short and in overall all studies have **one or more of the following drawbacks**: not using GDP per capita of the total population as dependent variable; or/and low R^2; or/and small samples; or/and unclear theory underneath the independent variables choice.

[1] Global Competitiveness Report, World Economic Forum

[2] World Competitiveness Yearbook, Institute for Management Development

Thus what is needed is a theory, simple (to be easy to interpret) and sensible (to pass the reasonable doubt test that results are not due to other variables).

But where to find such a theory[1]?

---

[1] As A. Banerjee and E. Duflo both MIT professors report in their book Good Economics for Hard Times (Penguin Random House 2019) "the bottom line is that there is no accepted recipe to make growth... happen... even among World Bank experts: in 2006, the World Bank asked the Nobel laureate Michael Spence to lead the Commission on Growth and Development (informally known as the Growth Commission). Spence initially refused, but convinced by the enthusiasm of his would-be fellow panelists, a highly distinguished group that included Robert Solow, he finally agreed. But their report ultimately recognized that there are no general principles, and no two growth episodes seem alike. Bill Easterly, not very charitably perhaps, but quite accurately described their conclusion: After two years of work by the commission of 21 world leaders and experts, and 11-member working group, 300 academic experts, 12 workshops, 13 consultations, and a budget of $4m, the experts' answer to the question of how to attain high growth was roughly: we do not know, but trust experts to figure it out" (William Easterly, "Trust the Development Experts—All 7 Billion", Brookings Institution, 2008, https://www.brookings.edu/opinions/trust-the-development-experts-all-7-billion/.)
As a side point it should be noted that as the best economists work in developed countries, eventually their main concern, what is most relevant for them, are stabilization and short term policies. And to a lesser degree economic growth in the long run.

3.2
What If Countries Were Companies?

There are no underdeveloped countries,
only undermanaged ones.

Peter F. Drucker

3.2.1 What if countries were companies?

Figure 3-5 indicates the turnover of the ten world largest companies. Many times greater than a high number of countries.

Figure 3-5

Ten largest world multinationals by revenue

Rank	Company	Revenue (Millions of Dollars)	Headquarters
1	Walmart	559.151	United States
2	State Grid	386.618	China
3	Amazon	386.064	United States
4	China National Petroleum	283.958	China
5	Sinopec Group	283.728	China
6	Apple	274.515	United States
7	CVS Health	268.706	United States
8	UnitedHealth	257.141	United States
9	Toyota	256.722	Japan
10	Volkswagen	253.965	Germany

Source: Fortune Global 500; 2021

And so, the question arises: since many multinationals are far larger than countries in terms of sales, e.g. Walmart (559 billion dollars), State Grid (387), Amazon (386), Apple (275), Toyota (257) or Volkswagen (254), **why not look at countries as diversified corporations**, where the government plays the role of the headquarters and the economic sectors that of divisions or departments?

In such a case the answer of what causes competitiveness is straightforward: the **quality of the business administration** areas: *strategy, marketing, human resources, R&D, operations, general management (organization, control and coordination mechanisms), finance/accounting, information systems and the administrative area (security, hygiene, etc.).*

That would explain differences in competitiveness and therefore in income per capita, among countries. And to test such an hypothesis **three** things are needed.

First, a way to **measure** a country's quality on the various business areas. Second, a large enough **sample**, both in terms of countries and years. And finally, a **statistical analysis** which passes the most important tests.

3.2.2   Operationalizing   the   business administration areas

Strategy is a concept originated in the military, meaning **where** to fight (compete), distinct from *tactics* which means *how* to do it.

In organizations the decision of where to compete respects the selection of **geographical areas, industries** and **segments**, which must be chosen according to three criteria: 1) *attractiveness* (rate of growth, margin and sales volume); 2) *synergy* (be it marketing or technological allowing for the sharing of distribution channels, salesforce, machinery, etc.); and 3) *competitiveness* (when a company's strengths match the key success factors—e.g. image in luxury brands, reliability in public works machinery since any malfunctions halts all work around, etc.).

Now, if a country's economy is totally closed to trade, its inhabitants are condemned to buy national goods regardless of their price and quality. Of their competitiveness.

However, when a country is open to foreign trade, consumers can and will buy goods, regardless of their origin and only **if** they are competitive.

And the more so, the less trade barriers exist, that is, the more *open* the internal market is.

Thus the larger the importance of trade (exports plus imports) in a country's GDP, the more a country must be competitive and **openness** can therefore be used as an indicator of competitiveness, one of the criteria of the quality of a strategy. The statistics will be supplied by the World Bank.

Marketing (pricing, advertising, sales promotion, etc.) is how companies attract consumers. However when monopolies, oligopolies, or firms with great market power prevail, marketing is much less needed as clients lack freedom of choice, being the alternative not to buy the product at all, something very hard when the good is of basic, first necessity.

So, the greater the **economic freedom**[1] in a country (an index developed by the non-governmental organization[2] Heritage Foundation), the better the marketing of its companies have to be.

Human resources management involves several tasks, such as staffing (to put the right person in the right place), creating incentive systems (to motivate), career planning (to retain the best employees) and two other areas which are always fundamental: 1) **instruction** (measured by the variables of quality and enrollment level of primary and higher education and training of the World Economic Forum) and 2) **selection**.

And here two characteristics are also paramount: **personal ethics** (the absence of character is destructive in organizations) and **work ethics** (effort, willingness to assume responsibility, spirit of initiative, openness to new ideas, acceptance of team work, willingness to help others, etc.). All translated into attitude which is a small thing that makes a great difference[3].

Personal ethics (character) can be operationalized by the *corruption perception index* of the NGO Transparency International and work ethics by the *global entrepreneurship index* (of the NGO Global Entrepreneurship and Development Institute) which evaluates risk acceptance, networking, opportunity perception and start-up skills.

---

[1] The degree of economic freedom in a country depends on three factors: 1) the level of taxation (which is coercive); 2) the presence of the state in the economy (which allows for no competition); and 3) the intensity of competition on the private markets (few oligopolies, etc.), being the latter of interest to us.

[2] Henceforth NGO.

[3] Winston Churchill.

General management (organization chart, objectives setting, control and coordination) is measured by the *world management survey, a study by Bloom et al.*[1], **operations** by *gross fixed capital formation* as a percentage of GDP[2] and the **quality of R&D department** by the *global innovation index*, created together by the Cornell and Insead universities and the World Intellectual Property Organization.

The quality of the **information systems management** and **finance/accounting** were supplied by the *World Economic Forum* survey and the **administrative area** which includes *hygiene* was operationalized by the *healthy life expectancy* according to the *World Health Organization*; *energy* by the respective variable of the *World Economic Forum*; and *security* by the *global peace index* of the NGO Institute for Economics and Peace.

Figure 3-6 presents the **nine** business administration areas, from strategy to the back office, how they are operationalized (measured) and the source of information (statistical data from official sources, indexes produced by NGOs or academic surveys).

---

[1] Nicholas Bloom, Raffaella Sadun, John M. Van Reenen, "Management as a Technology?", Harvard Business School Strategy Unit Working Paper No. 16-133, Stanford University Graduate School of Business Research Paper No. 16-27 (2017)

[2] The source is the World Bank.

Figure 3-6

The nine business administration areas, their operationalization and sources

BUSINESS ADMINISTRATION AREAS			
Areas (and subareas)		**Indicator / operationalization**	**Source**
1. **Strategy**		% exports + imports (trade) on GDP	World Bank
2. **Marketing**		Economic freedom index	Heritage Foundation
3. **Human resources**	Instruction	Instruction quality	World Economic Forum
	Selection — Personal ethics	Corruption perception index	Transparency International
	Selection — Work ethics	Global entrepreneurship index	Global entrepreneurship and development institute
4. **General management**		World management survey	Bloom et al survey
5. **Operations/production**		% gross fixed capital formation on GDP	World Bank
6. **Research & Development**		Global innovation index	Cornell University + Insead + World Intellectual Property Organization
7. **Information systems**		ICT adoption	World Economic Forum
8. **Finance/accounting**		Financial System	World Economic Forum
9. **Administrative area**	Hygiene	Healthy life expectancy	World Health Organization
	Security	Global Peace Index	Institute for Economics and Peace
	Energy	Electricity access and quality	World Economic Forum

Having found a way to measure the causal variables, that is the sources of growth, the next step is to decide upon how to collect data.

3.2.3 The sample

The collection of information should have **three** characteristics: *countries*; *years*; and *lag time*.

To allow for a multicultural analysis, the thirty three countries of figure 3-7 were selected as they 1) vary in wealth (some are OECD members, others not such as Nicaragua or Nigeria) and 2) there is available data for them to measure the quality of the nine business administration areas (for instance all countries were included in the world management survey by Bloom et al.)[1].

[1] Nicholas Bloom, Raffaella Sadun, John M. Van Reenen, "Management as a Technology?", Harvard Business School Strategy Unit Working Paper No. 16-133, Stanford University Graduate School of Business Research Paper No. 16-27 (2017)

Figure 3-7

The thirty three countries analyzed in the study

Country	OECD MEMBER
Argentina	No
Australia	Yes
Brazil	No
Canada	Yes
Chile	Yes
China	No
Colombia	Yes
Ethiopia	No
France	Yes
Germany	Yes
Ghana	No
Greece	Yes
India	No
Ireland	Yes
Italy	Yes
Japan	Yes
Kenya	No
Mexico	Yes
Mozambique	No
New Zealand	Yes
Nicaragua	No
Nigeria	No
Poland	Yes
Portugal	Yes
Singapore	No
Spain	Yes
Sweden	Yes
Tanzania	No
Turkey	Yes
United Kingdom	Yes
United States	Yes
Vietnam	No
Zambia	No

Also, to strengthen the analysis, chronological data from several years was used and, to make the obtaining of results more demanding, an homogeneous period was chosen: thus the years between the end of the subprime and the beginning of the Covid crisis were selected.

Finally, to reinforce causality, there is a lag time in the data years: the years of the independent variables of business administration areas precede the dependent one of national income per capita, by one year.

Thus data was collected for the years 2014 to 2018 for the business administration areas and 2015-2019 for the national income per capita.

With five years and thirty three countries (figure 3-7), one has a total of 165 observation points and the next step is to perform a statistical analysis on the data.

3.2.3 The regression analysis

The statistical analysis involved **three** sequential steps.

First the *Lasso technique*[1] was performed to reduce multicollinearity in the data, that is, the (co)relation among the independent variables, as countries which rated best in e.g. strategy tended also to excel in, say, marketing, operations or R&D.

Although that is something to be expected as the best companies tend to outperform competitors in several areas, multicollinearity affects the reliability of the estimation of the variables parameters, and so the Lasso technique was applied to eliminate the most (co)related variables which were: 1) operations/production; 2)

---

[1] Trevor Hastie, Robert Tibshirani, Martin Wainwright, "Statistical Learning with Sparsity: The Lasso and Generalizations", Chapman & Hall/CRC (2015).

finance/accounting; and 3) the administrative area (hygiene, security and energy).

The **second** phase was to apply the ordinary least squares technique to the remaining six business areas, namely: 1) strategy; 2) general management; 3) marketing; 4) human resources (training, work and personal ethics); 5) information systems and 6) R&D.

And **finally several tests** were performed to assess the adequacy of the statistical analysis and they included:

1) If a *linear* model could be used;
2) If the model was *homoscedastic*;
3) The absence of *autocorrelation* of residuals;
4) On the *normal distribution* of the residuals; and
5) The absence of *multicollinearity*. [1]

---

[1] That a *linear* regression model can be used is confirmed by diagrams where the 1) expected value of the dependent variable is a straight line function of each independent variable, holding the others fixed; 2) the slope of that line is not dependent on the values of the other variables; and 3) it can reasonably be assumed that the effects of different independent variables on the expected value of the dependent variable are additive.

Also, the regression model does not present *heteroscedasticity* (indicating low interval of variance of the parameters of each variable).

The eventual *statistical interdependence* of the errors and the *correlation between consecutive errors* is not an issue since the sample data is mostly cross-section (33 countries) and not time series (only five years of observations from 2014 to 2018). Also the requirement of the *normal distribution of errors* is unnecessary given the objective of minimizing the mean squared errors; and the fact that this study sample size is quite large (165 observations).

The model does present however a high degree of *multicollinearity*: the average value of the VIF (the ratio of one divided by one minus the R^2) for all independent variables is 9, well above the cut point of 5 for moderate correlation; also there are some independent variables which if regressed upon the others, present an R^2

The result is that the statistical analysis is compliant with all tests except multicollinearity. That means that in spite of the Lasso technique some degree of (co)relation remains among the independent variables.

It should be noted, however, that the existence of multicollinearity, which will be further discussed in the next section, does not affect the confidence of the overall results (the global impact of **all**, taken together, business administration quality on income per capita) which is very high at 90% level: only 10% of the variance in income per capita among the countries remains unexplained.

But, it does prevent evaluating with confidence the impact on income per capita of **each** individual variable. Whether, for instance, strategy is more or less relevant than management or marketing. What, although important, is not, anyway, our primary goal.

---

greater than that of regressing national income per capita on all independent variables; and the value of the t test for all parameters is almost always greater than two. Thus the estimated values of the parameters of each variable (in figure 3-8 of the next section) are not reliable.

3.3
The Results

In the short-term, opinions can replace facts;
but in the long run, no.

H. Maucher (former president of Nestle)

Figure 3-8 indicates the **parameters** of all variables, that is their **impact** on national income per capita. As expected all of them are positive (indicating a **positive** impact of a country's business administration areas on economic growth) and **five** out of eight are **statistically significant** at least at 5% level (indicating a very low probability that the parameters values are due to chance).

Figure 3-8

The variables, parameters, t test and significance level

Areas (and subareas)			Indicator / operationalization	Parameter	Significance level
1. Strategy			% exports + imports (trade) on GDP	89	0%
2. Marketing			Economic freedom index	163	No
3. Human resources	Instruction		Instruction quality	165	No
	Selection	Personal ethics	Corruption perception index	37	No
		Work ethics	Global entrepreneurship index	151	5%
4. General Management			World management survey	8468	5%
5. Research & Development			Global innovation index	279	5%
6. Information systems			ICT adoption	346	1%
$R^2 = 90\%$ (F test)					0%

But, and as referred, there remains the problem of multicollinearity, whose presence affects the confidence on the estimation of each parameter value per se, although *it does not affect*

Anyway, multicollinearity is something to be expected as better firms tend to have higher quality on several, and not in a single business administration area. The competitiveness of Walmart, Toyota, Amazon, Apple or Volkswagen is not due solely to its marketing, but also to the quality of its manufacturing, excellence in human resources management and so forth. The best firms tend to excel in most (if not in all) business areas.

And most important of all results obtained is the R^2 of **90%** of the regression model (which is statistically significant at 0% level).

That means that only **10%** of the variance in income per capita among 33 countries in figure 3-7 (from Argentina and Australia to Vietnam and Zambia) during the homogenous five years in between the (end of the) subprime crisis and the (beginning of the) Covid crisis year of 2020, is not explained by the quality of those countries firms in six business areas, namely: 1) *strategy*; 2) *marketing*; 3) *human resources* (instruction + personal ethics + work ethics); 4) *general management* (organization control and coordination mechanisms); 5) *R&D*; and 6) *information systems.*

Thus, the high income per capita variance explained (90%), the low number of causal variables (six) and the theory which led to their choice (countries seen as diversified companies), constitute a considerable improvement on previous empirical evidence of both the academic works analyzed in chapter 3.1 and on indexes such as those of the World Economic Forum or the Institute for Management Development which use hundreds of variables. All in opposition to the theory of this book: competitiveness depends on the quality of a country's business administration areas.[1]

---

[1] The latter Institute for Management Development index has 334 variables.

3.4
Conclusion

Please don't bring me opinions;
bring me facts.

(Label on the top of USA president F.D. Roosevelt's desk)

Economists have for long discussed the **sources** of economic growth, with disagreement fueled by the lack of decisive empirical evidence.

By opposition in the **business administration** area there is a far larger consensus. The theory, here, is that an organization's competitiveness is a function of the quality of its business areas: 1) strategy; 2) marketing; 3) human resources; 4) general management; 5) operations; 6) R&D; 7) information systems; 8) finance/accounting; and 9) administrative area (hygiene, security, energy).

The fact that many multinationals (from the UnitedHealth group to Toyota) are far larger than countries, raises the question: **what if one were to consider countries as large diversified companies**, whose competitiveness depends upon the quality of their business administration areas?

Under this perspective and evaluating the business functions with official data (e.g. from World Bank) in some instances, and indexes by NGOs (e.g. the Global Entrepreneurship and Development Institute) on others, or surveys performed by academics (Bloom et al.) still on others instances, one is able to explain **90%** of the income variance among **33** countries (from Argentina to Brazil, to Canada, etc. in figure 3-7) during the **five** years period in between the end of the subprime crisis and the start of the Covid recession.

Those results are not only significant but also solid, since in the linear regression model used 1) all variables parameters are positive, 2) most significant and the statistical analysis passes all tests of 3) homoscedasticity, residuals 4) normal distribution and 5) absence of autocorrelation; the exception being that—in spite of the Lasso technique and, as explained something to be expected—the data retains some degree of multicollinearity.

It is noteworthy that the results go beyond indicating that the richest countries have the best firms.

They demonstrate empirically that the wealthiest countries **are,** the best companies. The whole of the countries. The private sector. The public one. The social sector. The part of the population entering and leaving the active population (at different life phases).

All together. In human resources management (work ethics, instruction and personal ethics); strategy (operationalized by openness to trade that affects all including the input costs of the state and social sectors); information systems; the administrative area (hygiene, security and energy); and so on.

As a general conclusion one can thus say that the results bring a new meaning to the statement of *Peter Drucker,* founder of modern management, when he said that **there are no underdeveloped countries, only undermanaged ones**.

IV
Postface

"**Poverty** *is the worst form of* **violence**."

"*In a country well governed* **poverty** *is something to be ashamed of. In a country badly governed,* **wealth** *is something to be ashamed of.*"

M. Gandhi

Confucius

Singapore, the third wealthiest country in the world (the oil and gambling paradises of Qatar and Macao are the first two), has an income per capita **141** (one hundred forty one) times that of the world's poorest: Central African Republic.[1]

And Switzerland's income per capita (8th in the world) is **35** times that of Haiti[2] (the poorest outside Africa).

The top ten countries in the world have **59** times the per capita wealth of the bottom ten[3].

In Africa the income per capita of Botswana is **25** times that of African Central Republic and Burundi; **23** times that of the Republic of Congo; or **15** times that of neighboring Malawi.

In South America, **Chile**, the worst located country and with very few natural resources, has not only an income per capita 60%

---

[1] In dollars, Singapore income per capita is 100 345 and that of Central African Republic is 712 (source: IMF).

[2] Respectfully ranking 8th and 178th in the world with 65 000 and 1864 dollars of income per capita (source: IMF).

[3] Excluding those whose main export is oil, the top ten countries in GDP per capita are: Macao SAR, Singapore, Norway, Switzerland, Hong Kong SAR, Luxembourg, USA, San Marino, Netherlands and Iceland. And the world's bottom ten are Madagascar, Sierra Leone, South Sudan, Liberia, Mozambique, Niger, Malawi, Dem. Rep. of the Congo, Burundi and Central African Republic. The source is the IMF, 2019.

above that of Brazil (which is the richest in natural resources), but also Chile is by far the wealthiest south American country.

The European Union richest country is **Luxembourg**[1] where about 25% of its active population are Portuguese expatriates. **Portugal** however is the second poorest EU-15 country with only about **half** of Luxembourg's income per capita.

Thus the *simple* question: **why?** A simple question which has not been *easy* to answer for **two** reasons.

First, *empirical evidence* on the causes of economic growth has remained elusive with in the best of times little above *50%* the income variance among countries explained.

Still in other times when better results are achieved, they suffer from a lack of *trust* regarding the *choice of the causal variables*. Thus creating the fear of mere coincidental, spurious, relations. And consequently that what indeed influences income per capita are other unknown variables.

That is the problem that this book addressed resulting in being able to explain 90% of the income variance among countries.

The first step was to put aside what **doesn't work** in order to be able to focus on what really matters.

And so this book's first part demonstrated empirically that **Keynesianism**, due to globalization, stopped being relevant: more

---

[1] And after decreasing Luxembourg's income per capita with the corrections analyzed in chapter 2.1.

often than not there is no relation between public investment and prosperity.

Neither are **industrialization** policies productive: the wealthiest countries do not have a greater weight of industry in their economy.

Free trade and common policies within **economic blocks** also fail as both within the European Union and the United States, countries and states have diverged, not converged. The poorer improved, but the richer even more so making the difference between them greater.

And **funding** from the richer to the poorer has produced at best questionable results: after receiving 50 billion euros during a quarter of a century, to improve their competitiveness[1], Spain, Portugal and Greece, worsened not only in terms of their difference toward northern Europe, but also in competitiveness, economic freedom and transparency.

To make things worse (what cannot be measured cannot be managed—Peter Drucker), many countries and institutions evaluate economic progress with **gross domestic product per capita** which has become an obsolete statistic to be substituted by national income, what few do.

Then **location** is also far from a decisive factor as exemplified by Iceland and New Zealand. Both isolated and close to the (northern and southern) poles, they nevertheless rank 15th and 34th as the world wealthiest countries.

Climate, most specially temperature, is also a spurious explanation. At whatever temperature extreme. Although the year

---

[1] EU cohesion fund distinct from other EU funds on agriculture, fishing industry and human capital.

average temperature of Singapore is 32 degrees Celsius, it is the 3rd wealthiest country in the world.

At the other extreme that of Sweden is eight degrees, but it ranks 17th in income per capita, not to mention Finland, the world's 27th wealthiest country, whose southern part has an average year temperature of plus six degrees Celsius and in the north the year average is below zero.

Natural resources, except in the case of countries exceedingly small in population and extremely rich in oil, such as Qatar, Brunei and Kuwait, are neither a decisive factor: Venezuela has the largest world oil reserves, but ranks as 111th in income per capita, with Angola and Nigeria occupying the 131st and 136th positions respectively.

The case of Brazil is especially striking: 2nd in the world in iron ore, 4th in wood, 7th in tin, 9th in oil and 13th in gold. However, its income per capita is only average in South American terms, with Uruguay and Argentina faring 44% and 27% better, respectively.

On the subject of myths, a final aspect is worthwhile to mention: **genetics**. Portuguese productivity[1] is the second lowest in EU-15. About 70% of EU average. But with the Portuguese expatriates representing nearly 25% of its active population, Luxembourg has the highest EU productivity, 50% above EU average. Thus the productivity of the Portuguese in Luxembourg is 2,2 that of the Portuguese in… Portugal (see figure 4-1).

---

[1] GDP divided by employees (source: Ameco) with Ireland's values corrected to discount "mailbox multinationals". And data includes UK.

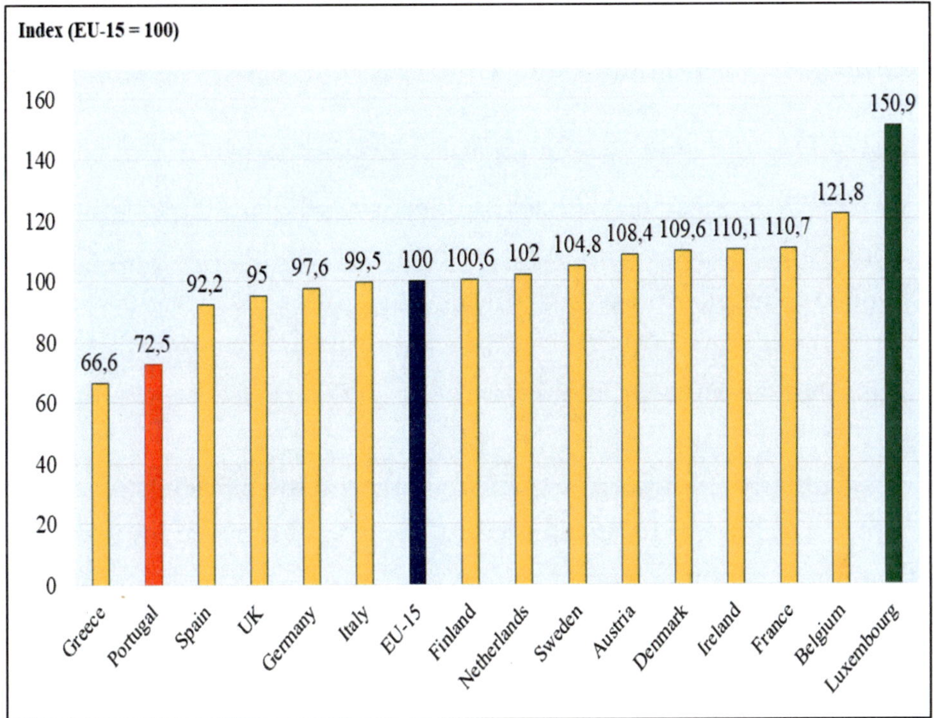

Source: AMECO, January 2022, European Commission.

Note: The value of Ireland's GDP stands for the Corrected National Income in order to take out the effect of subsidiaries of multinationals headquartered in this country only for fiscal reasons.

What that means is that if the Portuguese in Luxembourg were to come to Portugal to do the work of the residents, they would start their weekend on Wednesdays at 12:30 PM or annual holidays on June, the 25th.

So the first part of the book was dedicated to the **myths**. To what ain't so. But having done that, having put aside the false causes, it remained the central question of what are the **real** sources of growth, of competitiveness?

That was the focus of the book's **second part** and two facts helped to find the answer. First, such a problem *does not exist* in the area of organizations, of **business administration**. Second, there are many companies, from Walmart, to UnitedHealth, to Volkswagen, whose turnover is *far larger* than many countries.

And from those facts arise the question: why not look at countries as large diversified companies, with the government playing the role of headquarters, and test if among countries the decisive variables for competitiveness are the same as among organizations: the quality of marketing, strategy, etc.?

Such a question does not mean simply that the richest countries *have* the best firms (after all most of the world renown brands come from the developed world).

But that the wealthiest countries **are** the best companies, since the evaluation of the business administration areas was done for the countries as a whole (including the state and social sectors), and not only for the private sector.

And when that evaluation is done, **90%** of the economic growth is explained by **eight** variables:

- Work ethics (attitude translated into responsibility, effort, teamwork, discipline, punctuality, etc.);
- Personal ethics (trust, character);
- Training (including professional); and then the quality of the countries in terms of
- Marketing;
- Strategy;

-   General management (organization, control, and coordination mechanisms);
-   Information systems management; and finally
-   Innovation (R&D).

Although those were the results of a thorough statistical analysis performed on a large sample, they are nevertheless further subject to the **test** of a very simple question: what is the <u>one</u> example, a <u>single</u> one, of a country which ranking high in the above variables remains nonetheless poor? How many examples are there of great worldwide known, brands, from poor countries?

Or leaving aside oil paradises (such as Qatar, Brunei, UAE, Kuwait and Saudi Arabia), gambling heavens (as Macao) or the tax free San Marino, what is the example of a <u>sole</u> country which is rich while its population lacks 1) work and 2) personal ethics, 3) instruction and its companies are badly managed (in terms of 4) organization, 5) strategy and 6) information systems, while lacking 7) marketing and 8) innovation), that does not produce well-known brands?[1]

Neither is certainly the case of the countries which pertain to the list of the top twenty richest in the world[2]: Singapore (3rd), Norway (5th), Switzerland (8th), Hong Kong (9th), Luxembourg (10th), the USA (11th), Netherlands (12th), Iceland (15th), Taiwan (16th), Sweden (17th), Germany (18th), Australia (19th) and Austria (20th).

Those countries, in spite of being highly culturally diverse, from Switzerland to Iceland to Taiwan, they do share, have in common,

---

[1] Of course that the opposite argument, namely that oil and gambling paradises do not have these qualities, is not done here.

[2] Oil, gambling and tax heavens excluded.

what really matters for economic growth and prosperity. By opposition to the *myths*, the *facts*: the **quality of their business administration areas**.

Selected References

Although major works were quoted along the text, including providing complete footnotes references for them, it may nevertheless be useful for the reader to list all of them together. Both books and articles. So, by alphabetic order:

- Acemoglu, D. and Robinson, J. A. (2012) 'Why nations fail—the origins of power, prosperity and poverty', Crown Publishers.
- Alvaredo, F. Chancel, L. Piketty, T. Saez, E. and Zucman, G. (2018) 'World Inequality Report 2018: Executive Summary', *World Inequality Lab.*
- Appelbaum, B. (2019) 'The Economists' Hour—How the false prophets of free markets fractured our society', Little Brown and Company.
- Banerjee, A. V. and Duflo, E. (2019) 'Good economics for hard times', Penguin Random House.
- Barro, R. J. (1996) 'Determinants of Economic Growth: A Cross-Country Empirical Study', NBER Working Paper 5698, *National Bureau of Economic Research.*
- Benhabib, J. and Spiegel, M. M. (1994) 'The role of human capital in economic development evidence from aggregate cross-country data', *Journal of Monetary Economics*, **34**, 2, 143-73.

- Bloom, N., Sadun, R. and Van Reenen, J. M. (2017) 'Management as a Technology?', *Harvard Business School Strategy Unit Working Paper No. 16-133, Stanford University Graduate School of Business Research Paper No. 16-27.*

- De Long, J. F. (1988) 'Productivity Growth, Convergence, and Welfare: Comment', *American Economic Review*, **78**, 5, 1138-54. www.bradford-delong.com/2015/08/in-which-i-once-again-bet-on-a-substancial-growth-slowdown-in-china.html.

- Friedman, M. (1953) 'The methodology of positive economics', *Essays in positive economics*, Chicago: University of Chicago Press, 1, 3-43.

- Friedman, M. and Friedman, R. D. (1980) 'Free to choose: a personal statement', *Harcourt Brace Jovanovich.*

- Friedman, M. and Friedman, R. D. (1998) 'Two lucky people: memoirs', Chicago: University of Chicago Press.

- Fukuyama, F. (1995) 'Trust: The Social Virtues and the Creation of Prosperity', The Free Press.

- Gordon, R. J. (2016) 'The rise and fall of American growth: the U.S. standard of living since the Civil War', Princeton University Press.

- Grier, K. B. and Tullock, G. (1989) 'An empirical analysis of cross-national economic growth, 1951-1980', *Journal of Monetary Economics*, **24**, 2, 259-76.

- Hastie, T., Tibshirani, R. and Wainwright, M. (2015) 'Statistical Learning with Sparsity: The Lasso and Generalizations', Chapman & Hall/CRC.

- Kahneman, D. (2011) 'Thinking, Fast and Slow', Farrar, Straus and Giroux.

- Kavoussi, R. M. (1984) 'Export Expansion and Economic Growth—further empirical evidence', *Journal of Development Economica*, **14**, 241-50

- Keynes, J. M. (1936) 'The General Theory of Employment, Interest, and Money', Macmillan & Co.
- Landes, D. S. (1995) 'The Wealth and Poverty of Nations: Why Some Are So Rich and Some So Poor', Little Brown and Company.
- Lucas Jr., R. E. (1988) 'On the Mechanics of Economic Development', *Journal of Monetary Economics* 22, I, 3-42.
- Mankiw, N. G., Romer, D. and Weil, D. N. (1992) 'A contribution to the empirics of economic growth', *The Quarterly Journal of Economics*, **107**, 2, 407-37.
- Raghutla, C. (2020) 'The effect of trade openness on economic growth: Some empirical evidence from emerging market economies', *Journal of Public Affairs*, **20**, e2081.
- Romer, P. M. (1983) 'Dynamic competitive equilibria with externalities, increasing returns and unbounded growth (Ph.D.)', *The University of Chicago*.
- Romer, P. M. (1986) 'Increasing returns and long-run growth', *Journal of Political Economy*, **94**, 5, 1002-37.
- Romer, P. M. (1990) 'Human capital and growth: Theory and evidence', *Carnegie-Rochester Conference Series on Public Policy*, **32**, 251-86.
- Romer, P. M. (2008) 'Economic Growth', *The Concise Encyclopedia of Economics*, Indianapolis, Ind., Liberty Fund.
- Samuelson, P. A. (1964) 'Economics: An Introductory analysis', 6th ed., New York: McGraw-Hill, 807.
- Samuelson, P. A. (1976) 'Economics', 10th ed., New York: McGraw-Hill.
- Samuelson, P. A. and Nordhaus, W. D. (1989) 'Economics', 13th ed., New York: McGraw-Hill.
- Solow, R. M. (1956) 'A Contribution to the Theory of Economic Growth', *The Quarterly Journal of Economics*, **70**, 1, 65-94.

- Solow, R. M. (1957) 'Technical Change and the Aggregate Production Function', *The Review of Economics and Statistics*, **39**, 3, *The MIT Press,* 312-20
- Solow, R. M. (1963) 'Capital Theory and the Rate of Return', North-Holland Publishing Company.
- Solow, R. M. (1970) 'Growth Theory: an exposition', Oxford Clarendon Press.
- Solow, R. M. (2001) 'Applying Growth Theory across Countries', *The World Bank Economic Review*, **15**, 2, 283-8.
- Thaler, R. H. (2015) 'Misbehaving: The Making of Behavioral Economics', W. W. Norton & Co.
- Vogel, E. F. (1979) 'Japan As Number One: Lessons for America', Harvard University Press.
- Wanniski, J. (1989) 'The way the world works', *Polyconomics Inc.*
- Zhu, S. and Li, R. (2017) 'Economic complexity, human capital and economic growth: empirical research based on cross-country panel data', *Applied Economics*, **49**, 38, 3815-3828.